MW01029027

MISSION IN THE EARLY CHURCH

Mission in the Early Church

Themes and Reflections

Edward L. Smither

CASCADE *Books* · Eugene, Oregon

MISSION IN THE EARLY CHURCH
Themes and Reflections

Cascade Books
An Imprint of Wipf and Stock Publishers
199 W. 8th Ave., Suite 3
Eugene, OR 97401

www.wipfandstock.com

ISBN 13: 978-1-61097-521-6

Cataloguing-in-Publication data:

Smither, Edward L.

Mission in the early church : themes and reflections / Edward L. Smither.

xviii + 178 pp. ; 23 cm. Includes bibliographical references and index.

ISBN 13: 978-1-61097-521-6

1. Missions—History—Early church, approximately 30-600. 2. Church history—Primitive and early church, approximately 30-600. I. Title.

BV2073 S63 2014

Manufactured in the U.S.A.   4/22/2014

For my students

Contents

List of Illustrations   *vii*

Acknowledgments   *ix*

Abbreviations   *x*

Introduction   1

1 Backgrounds   7

2 Who Were the Missionaries?   29

3 Suffering   49

4 Evangelism   74

5 Bible Translation   91

6 Contextualization   109

7 Word and Deed   127

8 Church   148

Epilogue   165

Bibliography   167

Index   177

List of Illustrations

Figures

1   Mosaic floor of Sufetula (Sbeitla, Tunisia) baptistery showing the post-Consantinian *chi–rho* symbol (copyright © Marcus Brooks; used with permission)   21

2   Baptistery in the church at Hippo Regius (Annaba, Algeria)   33

3   Mosaic depicting Daniel in the lions' den, an inspiration to suffering North African Christians   52

4   Carthage ampitheatre where Felicitas and Perpetua and others were put to death   65

5   Chapel where Columba is believed to be buried at Iona   84

6   Facsimile of the Book of Kells at Iona   97

7   St. Martin's cross at Iona   120

8   Book of Kells page showing Christ (Wikimedia Commons)   123

9   Basilica of Peace at Hippo where Augustine preached   134

10   Mosaic of North African converted house   152

11   Sufetula (Sbeitla, Tunisia) baptistery (copyright © Marcus Brooks; used with permission)   157

Table

1   Early Christian Missionaries   35

Acknowledgments

Writing a book is never a one-person show and so there are many people to thank. As much of the thought for this book has emerged from classroom discussions over the last several years, I would first like to thank my students in church history and history of missions classes in Lynchburg and Columbia who have helped me to clarify my thoughts on early Christian mission. Further arguments from this work have been field tested and ironed out through papers given at the Evangelical Missiological Society, the Evangelical Theological Society Patristics group, and even at one conference at the University of Leuven (Belgium); so I am grateful for the feedback of colleagues present at those meetings. Speaking of colleagues, I wish to thank my teammates at Columbia International University, especially Mike Barnett, David Cashin, and Chris Little, who have been good sounding boards for parts of this work. I wish to also thank Marcus Brooks for allowing me to use his excellent photos from Sbeitla, Tunisia. I must also express a debt of gratitude to a number of scholars of missions history who have been an inspiration and model to me through their work. These include Dana Robert, Andrea Sterk, Samuel Moffet, Michael Green, Alan Kreider, Lamin Sanneh, Kenneth Scott Latourette, and especially Andrew Walls. Finally, I would like to thank my family—my wife Shawn and children Brennan, Emma, and Eve—for being the joy of my life and friendly reminders of when it's time to stop working and play some.

Abbreviations

ANF	Ante-Nicene Fathers
ESV	English Standard Version
FC	Fathers of the Church
NASB	New American Standard Bible
NPNF	Nicene Post-Nicene Fathers
WSA	Works of Saint Augustine

Introduction

MY AIM IN THIS BOOK is to begin a discussion about early Christian mission that will impact how we think about and approach mission today. By offering a faithful historical narrative and highlighting the innovative work of intercultural workers, I want to tell some of the story of early Christian mission from around AD 100 to 750—also known as the patristic period. The goal of this exercise is to offer meaningful reflection for the modern global evangelical church as it presses forward in mission.

Studies in the history of Christianity often focus on the development of Christian thought, key personalities, important events, and movements within the church. While these are worthy areas of emphasis, I prefer Justo Gonzalez's take on Christian history—that "the history of the church is the history of its mission."[1] Indeed, each Gospel writer (including Luke in Acts) remembered the following commands and promises as the last words spoken by the Lord to his disciples: "Make disciples of all the nations . . . Go into all the world and preach the gospel to all creation . . . As the Father has sent Me, I also send you . . . Repentance for forgiveness of sins would be proclaimed in His [Jesus'] name to all the nations . . . You will be my witnesses in Jerusalem, and in all Judea and Samaria, and even to the remotest part of the earth."[2] This mandate was to proclaim Christ—his person and his work (especially his death, burial, and resurrection)—and to persuade the nations to follow his life, example, and teachings.[3] More

1. Cited in Escobar, *Changing Tides,* 4.

2. Matt 28:19; Mark 16:15; John 20:21; Luke 24:47; Acts 1:8 (NASB); also Irvin and Sunquist, *History of the World Christian Movement,* 25; Marshall, "Who Were the Evangelists?," 256.

3. I am working from the broad definition that evangelism is proclaiming the person and work of Christ. For more on the essence of the message (*kerygma*) proclaimed by the apostles, see Dodd, *The Apostolic Preaching*; and Green, *Evangelism in the Early Church,* 76–115.

than mere parting words, these evangelical values were also at the center of Jesus' earthly ministry.[4] After three years of apprenticing with the Lord, the Twelve and the broader community of disciples[5] had also seized these convictions and the gospel spread, as early Christian history testifies. At the end of the second century, Tertullian (ca. 160–220) boasted to the Roman authorities in Carthage (North Africa): "We are but of yesterday, and we have filled every place among you—cities, islands, fortresses, towns, market-places, the very camp, tribes, companies, palace, senate, forum— we have left nothing to you but the temples of your gods."[6] Though Tertullian was given to exaggeration, the pagan Governor Pliny of Bithynia (in northern Asia Minor) was certainly not. In a letter to the Emperor Trajan in 112, he indicated that Christians were present in the towns and cities, and could be found on every level of society in his province.[7] The reality of the gospel traversing class lines—itself an indication of a mature church movement that was transforming culture—was acutely observed when the noblewoman Perpetua faced martyrdom alongside her servant Felicitas in Carthage in 203. In all, by the time of Constantine's rise to power in the early fourth century, there were around six million Christians in the Roman Empire alone—some 10 percent of the population—and the gospel had also spread eastward to places such as Edessa (Osroehene), Armenia, and Persia.[8] Indeed, early Christian history was the history of mission.

What do we mean by mission? Following the consensus of missiological thought in most traditions, I am persuaded that Christian mission flows from the mission of God (*missio Dei*) as "God is the one who initiates and sustains mission."[9] That is, God is a missionary God and he invites the church to participate in his redemptive work among the nations.[10] So, I define *mission* as "the divine activity of sending intermediaries . . . to speak or to do God's will so that God's purposes for judgment or redemption

---

4. Robert, *Christian Mission*, 11.

5. For a discussion on the relationship between the Twelve, the seventy, and the broader discipleship community, see Meier, *Marginal Jew*, 21; and Smither, *Augustine as Mentor*, 6.

6. Tertullian, *Apology* 37.4 (ANF 3).

7. Pliny, *Letter* 10.96, cited in Latourette, *History of the Expansion of Christianity*, 1:141; cf. Frend, *Martyrdom and Persecution*, 162–64. For more on Pliny's background and career, see Kalantzis, *Caesar and the Lamb*, 72–73.

8. Stark, *Rise of Christianity*, 6.

9. Moreau et al., *Introducing World Missions*, 17.

10. Cf. Gruder, *Missional Church*, 4–5.

are furthered."[11] *Missions* then is the specific work of the church and its *missionaries* to make disciples of all nations through evangelism, discipleship, church planting, and related ministries.[12] Following Escobar's definition, *missiology* is "an interdisciplinary approach to understand missionary action. It looks at missionary facts from the perspectives of the biblical sciences, theology, history, and the social sciences."[13] Thus, in offering an appraisal of early Christian mission, I will examine both the history of missions (strategies, methods, and approaches) and the work of missionaries in an effort to understand some of early Christian missiology. While my approach is historical, I will certainly interact with the early Christian narrative from a missiological point of view—one that is informed by contemporary, global perspectives. This is not to impose mission on history because, as church history is the history of its mission, it is quite reasonable that we read Christian history missionally.

Perhaps some may ask—at what point did mission become mission in the history of the church? Is it not anachronistic to refer to mission in the early church? Bosch is correct in asserting that in the patristic period "the Latin word *missio* was an expression employed in the doctrine of the Trinity, to denote the sending of the Son by the Father, and of the Holy Spirit by the Father and the Son."[14] However Robert argues: "The idea of 'mission' is carried through the New Testament by 206 references to the term 'sending.' The main Greek verb 'to send' is *apostollein*. Thus *apostles* were literally those sent to spread the 'Good News' of Jesus' life and message."[15] That is, mission has been central to the identity of the Christian movement since its inception. Christianity is a missionary faith. Referring to mission-related vocabulary, Bosch adds: "For fifteen centuries the church used other terms to refer to what we subsequently call 'mission': phrases such as 'propagation of the faith,' 'preaching of the gospel,' apostolic proclamation,' 'promulgation of the gospel,' 'augmenting the faith,' 'expanding the church,' 'planting the church,' propagation of the reign of Christ,' and 'illuminating the nations.'"[16] In short, though the Constantinian paradigm shift beginning

11. Larkin, *Mission in the New Testament*, 3.

12. Moreau et al., *Introducing World Missions*, 17; for more on what constituted a missionary in the early church, see Hvalvik, "In Word and Deed," 266–73.

13. Escobar, "Evangelical Missiology," 101.

14. Bosch, *Transforming Mission*, 228.

15. Robert, *Christian Mission*, 11.

16. Bosch, *Transforming Mission*, 228.

in the fourth century certainly brought confusion to an understanding of mission, it remained a central aspect of Christianity and we can certainly identify missionary motives and endeavors even when the term mission itself is not always used.

So, why study early Christian mission? Evangelical Protestants, the Christian tradition with which I most identify, are often led to believe that the history of missions began with William Carey in the late eighteenth century; hence, a reflective work on early church mission should challenge this idea and fill in some important gaps in our understanding of missions history. For a number of years, I have been teaching courses on missions history and have had to offer supplemental lectures on the early church period because of the lack of available scholarship. So, in many respects, this project has grown out of classroom lectures and discussions. My hope is that the present work will serve as a resource to professors and students as they consider the history of the church and its mission. On a personal note, I am privileged to work in two fields of study—early church history and missiology—and this project is an opportunity to combine these two passions.

Presently, there are several excellent books that address missions history. Stephen Neill's *A History of Christian Missions* is a comprehensive work that covers the history of Christianity to the mid-twentieth century; however, only around 10 percent of the book deals with the early church. Similarly, Ruth Tucker's *From Jerusalem to Irian Jaya: A Biographical History of Christian Missions* offers a colorful look at the lives of missionaries; yet, like Neill, it only briefly addresses early Christianity. Though Stephen Bevans' and Roger Schroeder's *Constants in Context: A Theology of Mission for Today* is a helpful volume on the history of missiology, their treatment of early church missiology is also limited. Eckhard Schnabel's two-volume *Early Christian Mission* is also a significant work; however, it largely focuses on mission in the New Testament and only the last section of volume two interacts with the post-first-century church. Finally, while Michael Green's celebrated work *Evangelism in the Early Church* does address the same period as the present work, it deals primarily with kerygmatic proclamation. Though mission cannot exist without verbal proclamation, the present study will examine early church mission from a broader and more comprehensive perspective. While these important books offer a significant point of departure for the present study, they also point to the need for it.

In the first chapter, the historical landscape of the early church from 100 to 750 will be laid out, including a brief summary of where the gospel spread. We will also consider how missions were affected by the fourth-century change in Christianity's official status—from illegal to official religion—and by political changes such as the fall of Rome and the rise of Islam. It should be noted that this chapter will not offer a comprehensive narrative and so, in some cases, the previously mentioned works on missions history should be consulted. In chapter two, we will explore the identities of the early church missionaries. In chapters three to eight, we will describe some factors and strategies that seemed to characterize mission during this period. These themes include suffering (chapter three), evangelism (four), Bible translation (five), contextualization efforts (six), ministry in Word and deed (seven), and the church (eight). Though the church can certainly be regarded as an outcome of mission, it will also be considered as a foundation of and means for mission. I will conclude the book with a final, reflective epilogue.

As this work aims to be a conversation with early church mission and missionaries, each chapter will include a relevant passage of Scripture as well as reflections where connections between early church and contemporary church practice can be made. Finally, I will close each chapter with some questions for reflection—points that will facilitate dialogue with Scripture and early church practice as the present global church moves forward in mission.

What are the limits of this study? As the period in question is vast and the places and peoples are diverse, it will be impossible to treat thoroughly each context of Christian mission. Thus, this work aims to serve as an introductory reflection on some prominent marks of Christian mission in the early church. Indeed, each chapter could eventually be expanded into a book-length project. Also, my intent is to focus on the history of mission as it has been defined. So, while political figures and developments will at times be unavoidable, this work is not concerned with the expansion of Christendom through political force but with the practical outworking of the *missio Dei* in the first eight and a half centuries through proclamation, service, and suffering. Finally, though the stated scope of the work is 100 to 750, at times some discussion of first-century mission will be included to provide a context.

Finally, this book is not primarily written for scholars; but rather for students of Christian history studying at the undergraduate and initial

graduate level. As I have endeavored to make this an accessible and read-
able work, my hope is that it will serve the church, including those with
no background in historical studies. I am persuaded that every follower
of Christ should engage with our Christian memory as we strive to be the
people of God on mission today.

1

Backgrounds

IT SEEMS IMPOSSIBLE TO UNDERSTAND Martin Luther's (1483–1546) doctrine of justification by faith—a central aspect of his theology and a hallmark of the Protestant Reformation—without first understanding something of his personal background. His father Hans, who worked in the mining industry, was known for being a harsh disciplinarian and also for his ambition to see his son receive a quality education that would lead to a successful career.[1] Naturally, he was happy when Luther began studies in law at the University of Erfurt in 1501; but he had quite the opposite reaction when his son abandoned law and entered an Augustinian monastery a few years later. As a monk, Luther nearly destroyed his digestive system through rigorous fasting, he trembled with fear at the task of presiding over the Eucharist, and he became obsessed with confession—doubting his sincerity in confession and worrying about committing more sin. Eventually, his monastic mentor Johannes Staupitz encouraged him to "sin boldly" and only come to confession when Luther had *really* sinned. Having disappointed an abrasive father and struggling as a monk, Luther began to despise the God he was attempting to serve. Then, in the course of study, he happened upon Paul's words in Romans 1:17, "For in it the righteousness of God is revealed from faith for faith, as it is written, 'The righteous shall live by faith.'"[2] Discovering God's grace and salvation through faith,

1. Marty, *Martin Luther*, 3.

2. Unless otherwise indicated, all Scripture reference are taken from the English Standard Version (ESV).

Luther related, "Here I felt that I was altogether born again and had entered paradise itself through open gates."[3] While Luther's family life and early monastic experience would not facilitate him grasping the beauty of God's grace, certainly he savored it that much more because of this background. Indeed, it seems impossible to understand Luther's doctrine of justification without having an understanding of his personal background.

Any decent commentary on a book of Scripture will first include a section on background questions. Who was the author? The audience? From where was the book written? Where did the audience live? What was their history and what were their issues? What was the author's purpose in writing? A thrilling investigation for some students, others quickly rush through the background matter to get on to the weightier matters of exegesis. Yet, hopefully, the latter group will eventually learn that some of the most exciting exegetical discoveries come through a useful background study of the context.

If this book is a commentary on mission in the early church, then the present chapter serves as that necessary background check that will surely unlock some mysteries and shine light on the practice and thought of early Christian mission. We will begin by asking, briefly so, where were they Christians in the world in the first eight and a half centuries?[4] This first question will largely address the origins and initial development of Christianity in each region. Second, what were the political and social contexts in which missionaries labored? Finally, what were the currents of thought—religions, philosophies, and worldview—that the church encountered in its missionary expansion?

Where Were They Christians?

From the New Testament evidence—especially from Luke but also through Paul's letters—the gospel spread significantly through the missionary work of the Apostle Paul. While the promised areas of Jerusalem, Judea, and Samaria had been touched,[5] Antioch of Syria was also evangelized and

---

3. Dillenger, *Martin Luther: Selections*, 11.

4. For a more thorough presentation of the geographic expansion of Christianity, see Latourette, *History of the Expansion of Christianity*, vols. 1–2; and Irvin and Sunquist, *History of the World Christian Movement*.

5. Acts 1:8.

became an important sending church for Paul and his companions.[6] From there, they carried out mission work on the islands of Cyprus, Malta, and Crete; in Asia Minor and Asia between Tarsus and Macedonia; to Greece, Italy, and Rome; and probably Spain.[7] In general, Paul's first-century ministry progressed in a westward direction from Antioch toward Spain.

Expansion West

In the centuries that followed, Christian mission continued to flow westward from Jerusalem and Antioch primarily within the Roman Empire. Ironically, the region of Palestine remained largely non-Christian until the reign of Constantine in the fourth century and most ministry efforts were focused on the Jews. In neighboring Phoenicia, there was a strong church in the city of Tyre; however, Christian communities were largely Greek-speaking and confined to the cities.[8]

Prior to becoming Paul and Barnabas' sending church, Antioch of Syria was evangelized in the first century amid suffering and it is remembered for being the first place where followers of Jesus were called Christians—a pejorative name given by the pagan majority.[9] Antioch was a cosmopolitan center characterized by Jewish, Hellenistic, and Roman influences,[10] which would contribute to it being an important locale for biblical interpretation and for sending intercultural missionaries toward the West and the East. By the fourth century, the population probably included close to a half million residents and there was a significant Christian population.[11]

Within Asia Minor, Governor Pliny's letter of 112 testified to the growing communities of Christians in Bithynia while Pontus and much of Cappadocia were reached through the efforts of Gregory Thaumaturgus (ca. 213–270) by the end of the third century. In Asia, the cities of Smyrna and Ephesus, both within the province of Phrygia, continued to have a growing Christian presence. The martyred bishop Polycarp (d. 156) was

---

6. Acts 11:19–27; 13:1–3.

7. Latourette, *History of the Expansion of Christianity*, 1:68–86.

8. Neill, *History of Christian Missions*, 28–29; Latourette, *History of the Expansion of Christianity*, 1:86–87.

9. Acts 11:26.

10. Irvin and Sunquist, *History of the World Christian Movement*, 28–29.

11. Neill, *History of Christian Missions*, 29; Latourette, *History of the Expansion of Christianity*, 1:87.

a key missionary to Smyrna in the first half of the second century, while his mentor John the Evangelist apparently ministered in Ephesus in the latter half of the first century.[12] Of course, Justin Martyr's (ca. 100–165) famous public debate with the Jewish thinker Trypho took place in Ephesus around 135.[13]

Despite becoming the largest community of Christians in the western Roman Empire by the third century, the origins of the church at Rome are unclear. While claims that Peter and Paul founded the church lack support, the first indication of Christianity in the city probably comes through the historian Suetonius who recorded that Emperor Claudius had dealt with an uprising of the followers of *Chrestus* (perhaps a misspelling of *Christos* or "Christ") around the year 50.[14] The church was a Greek-speaking community for most of the second century, an indication that the movement had largely taken hold among the lower classes, until Bishop Victor (d. 199) introduced Latin as the language of worship in 189. Some have estimated that by the middle of the third century, there were as many as 30,000 Christians in Rome—a figure extrapolated from the large number of clergy serving the church.[15]

Similarly, the beginnings of the church in Gaul are difficult to detect. Though some traditions claim that Paul's disciple Crescens was an early evangelist to the region,[16] the gospel probably came from Syria, Asia, and Asia Minor via Christian merchants. Indeed, Irenaeus (ca. 115–200), bishop of Lyon until 200, was initially set apart to minister to a congregation of Greek-speaking immigrants in the city. Further, many of the Christians who suffered in the persecutions of 177 were not of Gallic origin.[17] As the church expanded, bishops were probably appointed in Cologne and Mainz by 185, and churches were established in Arles, Rouen, Bordeaux, and Paris by the fourth century.[18]

Though we are unable to confirm if Paul actually ministered in Spain, both Tertullian and Cyprian (195–258) make mention of Spanish churches

12. Irvin and Sunquist, *History of the World Christian Movement*, 66.

13. Latourette, *History of the Expansion of Christianity*, 1:87–90.

14. Irvin and Sunquist, *History of the World Christian Movement*, 74–75.

15. Eusebius, *Church History* 6.43.6; Neill, *History of Christian Missions*, 29–31; Latourette, *History of the Expansion of Christianity*, 1:94–95.

16. Crescens is mentioned in 2 Tim 4:10.

17. Frend, *Martyrdom and Persecution*, 2.

18. Latourette, *History of the Expansion of Christianity*, 1:97–100.

in their third-century writings.[19] Also, in the acts of the Council of Elvira in the early fourth century, some thirty-six Spanish churches are listed.[20]

Though some legends claim that Paul and even Joseph of Arimathea were early catalysts in evangelizing Britain, and Tertullian alludes to Christians in the region by the early third century,[21] the first indisputable evidence for a British church comes from the acts of the Council of Arles in 314 in which bishops from London and York were present.[22] By 400, the Briton people of Roman Britain appear to have been evangelized; however, the Anglo-Saxons were largely neglected until the late sixth century and the ministry of Augustine of Canterbury (d. 604).[23] In the eighth century, English monks were catalysts for reaching the Saxons of Germany.

Despite its geographical proximity to Roman Britain, Ireland was never part of the Roman Empire. Christianity came to the Celts in the fifth century primarily through the work of the famous missionary-bishop Patrick (ca. 387–ca. 461). As a result of his nearly thirty years of ministry, much of Ireland was evangelized, which will be discussed more in the next chapter.[24] In the sixth century, Celtic missionary monks left Ireland to evangelize Scotland, and what is now Switzerland and France.

Prior to the lives and ministries of Clement (ca. 150–ca. 215) and Origen (ca. 185–254) of Alexandria, little is known about the origins of Egyptian Christianity. Eusebius, citing Clement, presented the traditional claim that the church had been planted by Mark the Evangelist.[25] As Alexandrian Christians were challenged to articulate their faith in a Gnostic milieu, the church opened a catechetical school, led by Pantaenus (d. 200), Clement, and later Origen, to offer doctrinal training to new believers. While the

19. Tertullian, *Against the Jews* 7; Cyprian, *Letter* 67.

20. Neill, *History of Christian Missions,* 31; Latourette, *History of the Expansion of Christianity*, 1:96–97.

21. Tertullian, *Against the Jews* 7; Thomas, *Christianity in Roman Britain*, 42–43.

22. The most thorough ancient source for a window into British Christian history is Venerable Bede's eighth-century work *Ecclesiastical History of the English People.* For a survey of the extent of Christianity in Roman Britain, see Thomas, *Christianity in Roman Britain*, 267–74.

23. Neill, *History of Christian Missions,* 31–32; Latourette, *History of the Expansion of Christianity*, 1:100.

24. Neill, *History of Christian Missions,* 49–50; Latourette, *History of the Expansion of Christianity*, 1:216–22.

25. Eusebius, *Church History* 2.16. This position, traditionally held by Egyptian Coptic Christians, has been affirmed by Thomas Oden in his recent work *The African Memory of Mark.*

churches in Alexandria were Greek-speaking, other Egyptian Christians were Coptic in language and culture, including Pachomius (ca. 290–ca. 346) and other pioneers of Egyptian monasticism.[26]

In assessing the spread of Christianity in the Roman Empire, Neill asserts that "it was . . . in the parts . . . today called Tunis and Algeria that the gospel most rapidly took hold."[27] The great irony is that, like Rome, the North African church had anonymous origins. Archaeological evidence suggests that there were communities of Christians in Cyrene (near modern Benghazi) by the end of the first century and in Hadrumetum (Sousse) by the mid-second century. The first actual written account of North African Christianity came from a court case in Carthage in 180 in which twelve believers were executed. As the North African church developed, it would be shaped by capable theologians such as Tertullian, Cyprian, and Augustine of Hippo (354–430).[28]

Expansion East

In recent years, scholars such as Irvin and Sunquist (*History of the World Christian Movement*), Moffett (*A History of Christianity in Asia*), Cragg (*The Arab Christian*), and Jenkins (*The Lost History of Christianity*) have helpfully reminded western Christians of the rich and colorful history of early Christian communities in the East, especially in those regions outside of the Roman Empire.[29] As the gospel expanded West from Antioch, it also ventured eastward to the Kingdom of Osrhoene and its capital Edessa. Though Osrhoene would come under Roman control by the early third century, this Syriac-speaking church had been nurtured by the Antioch church in the second century until a bishop was set apart around 200. Though Eusebius' claim that King Abgar of Edessa corresponded with Jesus during the Lord's lifetime has not found general acceptance, this account does show that the Syrians were surely exposed to the gospel well before the end of the second

26. Neill, *History of Christian Missions*, 32–33; Latourette, *History of the Expansion of Christianity*, 1:91.

27. Neill, *History of Christian Missions*, 34.

28. A helpful introduction to early African Christianity is Decret's, *Early Christianity in North Africa*.

29. On the other hand, Neill does not help matters when he titles chapter two of *History of Christian Missions* as merely "The Conquest of the Roman World, A.D. 100–500," as if Christian expansion were only limited to the Roman Empire in this period.

century.[30] In the fourth century, the Syrian church was strengthened by the work of its greatest theologian Ephraem (306–373), who theologized in the Syrian context through preaching and writing hymns.[31]

The Christian movement in Persia and Mesopotamia probably spread from Edessa in the second and third centuries through merchants and even through Christians who had been captured by the Persians. By 225, some twenty churches had been established in the Tigris-Euphrates Valley bordering Persia. One of these communities converted a house into a small church building around 232 at Dura-Europos on the Tigris River—one of the earliest excavated church structures from the early Christian period.[32] By 285, the first Persian bishop had been set apart and by the beginning of the fifth century, there was a recognizable network of churches and bishops in the region.[33]

Christianity probably penetrated Armenia through the ministry of Christians from neighboring Cappadocia and Syria.[34] The most celebrated missionary in the third century was Gregory the Enlightener (ca. 240–332). What makes Armenia unique in early Christian history is that following the conversion of King Tiridates, who was reportedly healed and later baptized by Gregory, Christianity was declared the national religion of Armenia.[35] This move represents the initial steps toward a Christendom paradigm, which will be discussed in more detail shortly.

The initial evangelization of India has been the subject of much speculation, especially regarding the alleged mission of Thomas. Though the specific details of mission cannot be confirmed, there is no doubt that there was a Christian presence in India by the third century.[36] In terms of church expansion, it is likely that the Indian churches were an extension of the church in Persia and were overseen by its leadership. One of the signers of

30. Eusebius, *Church History* 1.13; also Moffet, *History of Christianity in Asia*, 1:44–50; Neill, *History of Christian Missions*, 42–44; Irvin and Sunquist, *History of the World Christian Movement*, 57–61.

31. Irvin and Sunquist, *History of the World Christian Movement*, 197–98.

32. Latourette, *History of the Expansion of Christianity*, 1:103–105.

33. Moffet, *History of Christianity in Asia*, 1:117–38.

34. Wilken, *First Thousand Years*, 230.

35. Moffet, *History of Christianity in Asia*, 1:118–19; Neill, *History of Christian Missions*, 47–48; Latourette, *History of the Expansion of Christianity*, 1:106–106; Wilken, *First Thousand Years*, 229–30.

36. Moffet, *History of Christianity in Asia*, 1:24–39; cf. Wilken, *First Thousand Years*, 244–45.

the Nicene Creed of 325 was Bishop John of Persia who apparently signed on behalf of the churches of Persia and India.[37]

In one sense, the gospel penetrated Arabia very early because this was where Paul first preached following his conversion.[38] Despite this, we know very little about Christianity in Arabia before the fourth century. It seems that Arabs were most exposed to the gospel through the witness of Roman and Persian believers. The first known churches were established in what is now Qatar, while another bishop who ministered to Bedouin Arabs was present at the Council of Nicaea in 325. Finally, a number of fourth-century Arab monarchs embraced Christianity and invited missionaries to come and teach their people.[39]

Though Luke records Phillip baptizing an Ethiopian eunuch who served in the court of Queen Candace, scholars struggle to make a historical connection between that encounter and the origins of the church in Ethiopia.[40] The most reliable account for the beginnings of the Ethiopian church date to the early fourth century as two youths from Tyre named Frumentius and Aedesius were traveling with their teacher down the Red Sea when their ship was attacked and they were sold into slavery. After gaining favor with the authorities and being allowed to go free, Frumentius (d. ca. 383) chose to return to Ethiopia and is remembered for leading the royal family to faith in Christ, with starting new churches, and ordaining priests among other ministries. Finally, in 347, Frumentius was set apart as bishop for Ethiopia by Athanasius of Alexandria (ca. 300–373).[41]

While Chinese silk was available for purchase in Mediterranean markets before the third century, meaning Chinese merchants were probably interacting with Christians, there is no evidence for a Christian presence in China until the seventh century when the Chinese emperor favorably received Nestorian monks. As we will see, it was Nestorian Christians that spread Christianity along the Silk Road between Persia and China in the seventh and eighth centuries.[42]

---

37. Irvin and Sunquist, *History of the World Christian Movement*, 113–14.

38. Gal 1:15–17.

39. Moffet, *History of Christianity in Asia*, 1:273–75; Cragg, *The Arab Christian*, 31–48.

40. Acts 8:27.

41. Irvin and Sunquist, *History of the World Christian Movement*, 216–18; Wilken, *First Thousand Years*, 215–16.

42. Irvin and Sunquist, *History of the World Christian Movement*, 257; Moffet, *History of Christianity in Asia*, 1:287–314.

Finally, though located to the North and West of Antioch, the Gothic peoples certainly resided outside of the Roman Empire. In fact, it was these warring Germanic peoples from north of the Danube that overthrew Rome in the fifth century. Christianity first came to the Goths in the third and fourth centuries through the testimony of slaves—Cappadocian Christians captured by the Goths. The most famous missionary to the Goths, Ulfilas (ca. 311–ca. 383) was born to Cappadocian and Gothic parents. A moderate Arian, Ulfilas was set apart in 340 as bishop to the Goths by another Arian bishop, Eusebius of Nicomedia (d. 341).[43]

Ulfilas, an Arian Missionary

In his letter commemorating the life and ministry of his mentor Ulfilas, Auxentius describes Ulfilas' theology: "In both his sermons and his tractates he showed that a difference does exist between the divinity of the Father and of the Son, of God unbegotten and God only-begotten, and that the Father is for his part the creator of the creator, while the Son is the creator of all creation; and that the Father is God of the Lord while the Son is God of the created universe . . . The Holy Spirit he furthermore declared to be neither Father nor Son, but made by the Father through the Son before all things . . . Now since there exists only one unbegotten God and there stands under him only one only-begotten God, the Holy Spirit our advocate can be called neither God nor Lord."[44]

Given that Ulfilas denied the eternality and equality of the Father, Son, and Holy Spirit—clearly articulated in the Creeds of Nicaea (325) and Constantinople (381)—what effect did that have on the gospel he proclaimed? Did his gospel result in true conversions and transformation among the Goths? As we contemplate mission today, how important is our theology to our mission practice?

Political and Social Contexts

Given this survey of Christianity's spread, let us also briefly describe the political and social contexts in which the church expanded and missionaries labored. For simplicity's sake, we will consider three major periods: from the end of the first century to the emergence of Constantine (100–312); from Constantine's reign to the rise of Islam (312–610); and finally through

---

43. Irvin and Sunquist, *History of the World Christian Movement,* 179–80.

44. Auxentius of Durostorum, *Letter on the Life and Work of Ulfila, Apostle of the Goths* 27, 30–31, cited in Coakley and Sterk, eds., *Readings in World Christianity,* 103.

the Islamic period until the middle of the eight century (610–750). In each period, we will inquire about the status of Christians and the political and social regard for them—background that will frame discussions in the forthcoming chapters.

The Pre-Constantinian Period

The story of early Christianity was characterized by sporadic periods of discrimination and suffering from its beginnings until well into the fourth century. Of course, the movement's founder, Jesus of Nazareth, and its earliest missionaries—most of the Twelve and Paul—died as martyrs. Irvin and Sunquist helpfully observe, "the earliest Christian missionaries from Jerusalem went out as refugees and victims of persecution . . . these first Christians had expansionist tendencies without worldly power."[45] In 64–65, the Emperor Nero (15–68) persecuted Christians in Rome, while Domitian (51–96) probably did the same toward the end of the first century.[46]

From the second to early fourth century, followers of Jesus were met with discrimination and, at times, even violence. While it would be inaccurate to assert that persecution was constant or that the government—especially within the Roman Empire—was largely responsible, most actions against Christians were carried out on a local level.[47] In many cases, persecution was initiated by pagan mobs—angry at the Christian impiety that was dividing families and threatening society—that dragged Christians before local governors who ruled against the accused.[48] As many governors were charged with administrating vast territories, their judgments were often made hastily and in the interest of maintaining order.[49] It seems that Polycarp (156) and Christians in Lyon (177) and Alexandria (248) were victimized within this scenario. This also provides a context for understanding Pliny's appeal to Emperor Trajan in 112 for advice in dealing with accused Christians as he posed such questions as: Should people be

---

45. Irvin and Sunquist, *History of the World Christian Movement*, 26.

46. Guy, *Introducing Early Christianity*, 50–51.

47. Wilken, *First Thousand Years*, 65; also Moss, *Ancient Christian Martyrdom*, 12; and Kalantzis, *Caesar and the Lamb*, 25.

48. Paul Parvis, "Justin Martyr," 5–6; also Fox, *Pagans and Christians*, 423; and Kalantzis, *Caesar and the Lamb*, 11.

49. Guy, *Introducing Early Christianity*, 51–52; cf. Moss, *Ancient Christian Martyrdom*, 12.

treated differently according to age? Does recanting constitute a pardon? Is merely professing to be a Christian a crime? Trajan famously responded: "You have adopted the proper course . . . in your examination of the cases of those who were accused to you as Christians, for indeed nothing can be laid down as a general ruling involving something like a set form of procedure. They are not to be sought out; but if they are accused and convicted, they must be punished."[50] So if Christians were not to be sought out, how could they eventually be convicted and punished? Certainly, Trajan's ambiguous response—the official imperial policy from the early second century until the mid-third—contributed to further mob-instigated discrimination and violence.

Though persecution against Christians was largely carried out on a local level, there were some Roman emperors that initiated campaigns against the movement. In 202, Septimius Severus (145–211), the first Roman emperor from Africa, enacted a law forbidding conversion to Judaism and Christianity.[51] While this measure may have been taken to suppress the influence of Judaism, Christianity, or Montanism within the empire, it may have also been due to Severus' annoyance at the rapid spread of Christianity in Africa.

The first imperial persecution was carried out by Decius (ca. 201–251) beginning in 249.[52] Ironically, during the fifteen years prior, particularly during the reign of Emperor Phillip the Arab (244–49), Christians had enjoyed peace and some freedom to worship in parts of the empire. As Decius wanted to reform Rome and renew traditional pagan piety, it was necessary to root out what he perceived to be an atheistic sect.[53] In 249, an initial decree was given ordering all church leaders to offer sacrifices to the Roman deities and to lead their congregations to do the same. Though some leaders complied, others who resisted the order—including Bishops Fabian of Rome, Babylas of Antioch, and Alexander of Jerusalem—were put to death. In 250, the initial decree was followed by a universal order to sacrifice and administrators were brought into every province to oversee the process. Those who obeyed were dubbed "sacrificers" (*sacrificati*) and received a certificate (*libellus*), while other Christians managed to avoid

50. Pliny, *Letter* 10.97, cited in Stevenson, *A New Eusebius*, 16.

51. Frend, *Martyrdom and Persecution*, 238–42.

52. For a thorough discussion of Decius' campaign, see Frend, *Martyrdom and Persecution*, 285–323; also Wilken, *First Thousand Years*, 67–71.

53. Cf. Kalantzis, *Caesar and the Lamb*, 149.

the pagan ritual through bribing officials; however, they also received a certificate.[54] When Decius was killed in battle against the Goths in 251, this effectively ended the empire-wide suppression of Christianity. However, these circumstances raised some critical soteriological and ecclesiological questions for the church on the nature and consequences of apostasy. Cyprian's two treatises, *On the Lapsed* and *On the Unity of the Church*, were developed in this context.

Though Valerian (ca. 193–ca. 260) came to power in 253, he did not renew the imperial persecution until 257. In the first edict, he attempted to enforce a universal sacrifice by first ordering church leaders to honor the Roman cult. At the same time, worship assemblies and Christian funerals were banned. As the first order was largely ineffective, a second was given in 258 that ordered the execution of clergy, the confiscation of church members' property, the execution of resistant laymen, and a purging of the Roman Senate of all Christians. In 259 or 260, Valerian was killed in battle against the Persians and his son and successor Gallienus (ca. 218–268) issued an act of toleration in 261, which began a period of about forty years of peace for Christians in the empire.

Nearly twenty years into his reign, Diocletian (244–311) also wanted to return Rome to its traditional religion. Initially resistant to suppressing the church because his wife, daughter, and some key advisors were apparently Christians, Diocletian was eventually convinced by his subemperor Galerius (ca. 260–311) that this was the best course of action.[55] The first of four edicts was given in 303 in which churches were closed, worship assemblies banned, Scriptures were seized, and influential Christians in society were deprived of their civil rights. In the second edict, all clergy were forced to sacrifice or face imprisonment. In the third, clergy were again ordered to sacrifice or undergo torture or even execution. Finally, in the fourth edict, all citizens in the empire were commanded to sacrifice or face death. In the last instance, Diocletian's own family and counselors became victims of the order. In 305, Diocletian and Maximian (ca. 250–ca. 310), Diocletian's co-emperor in the West, abdicated their thrones. Constantius (250–306), Maximian's successor in the West and also the father of Constantine (ca. 274/288–337), put an end to Christian persecution in his domain when he came to power. However, Galerius continued to carry out the official policy in the eastern part of the empire until 311. The Great Persecution came to

---

54. Ibid.

55. Frend, *Martyrdom and Persecution,* 351–92.

an end in 311 when Galerius issued the Edict of Nicomedia from his death-bed. Despite his ongoing feelings of irritation toward the sect, the emperor effectively restored to the church the rights given in Gallenius' act of tolera-tion of 261, and even requested that Christians pray for the welfare of the empire: "Therefore, in view of this our clemency, they [Christians] are in duty bound to beseech their own god for our security, and that of the state and of themselves, in order that in every way the state may be preserved in health and they may be able to live free from anxiety in their own homes."[56]

As we have established the narrative and pattern of discrimination against Christians in the Roman Empire until the rise of Constantine, let us pose one further question: from a Roman perspective what were the specific charges against Christians that merited these actions? First, the Christians were accused of a general impiety. By failing to honor the many deities of the Roman pantheon, which often included the emperor him-self, Christians were accused of atheism—worshipping a god that they could not see.[57] It was believed that such impiety would ultimately anger the gods who would then remove their protection from Rome. Tertullian remarked: "They think the Christians the cause of every public disaster, of every affliction with which the people are visited. If the Tiber rises as high as the city walls, if the Nile does not send its waters up over the fields, if the heavens give no rain, if there is an earthquake, if there is famine or pestilence, straightway the cry is, 'Away with the Christians to the lion!'"[58] Though sarcastic, Tertullian's remarks do seem to capture the motivations of the pagan mobs as well as some emperors whose religion was certainly influenced by economic and military uncertainties. In short, in the mindset of the Romans, to be Roman was to be pagan.[59] In the midst of the Vandal conquest of Rome in the early fifth century, when the empire was officially Christian, many pagans blamed Christian impiety for the collapse of the empire, which was the occasion for Augustine to write his magnum opus, *The City of God.*

Within this pagan religious framework, the Roman government le-gally condemned Christianity in the pre-Constantine period for being an illegal sect (*religio illicita*). This status was due to the movement's exclusive

---

56. Cited in Eusebius, *Church History* 8.17.9 (all translations of Eusebius are from NPNF 2:1).

57. Fox, *Pagans and Christians,* 425–26.

58. Tertullian, *Apology,* 40.

59. Cicero, *On the Nature of the Gods* 1.2.4.

religious claims and rejection of the Roman pantheon's plurality of gods. Because they worshipped a god they could not see, Christians were considered atheists. Because of Roman misunderstandings regarding the Eucharist and agape feasts, the Christians were accused of cannibalism and sexual immorality—charges that Justin Martyr answered in his *First Apology*.[60] Finally, Christians were an illegal sect because they were considered a new religion. Though Jews were discriminated against by some emperors, they were never reduced to this illegal status because of their antiquity.

Constantine and Imperial Christianity

The direction of global Christianity took a drastic turn on the eve of Constantine's battle with Maxentius at Milvian Bridge in 312. According to conflicting reports from Eusebius and Lactantius, Constantine saw a sign in the sky—either the chi-rho labarum symbol or a cross—and was promised victory in battle.[61] He did emerge victorious and through this encounter was apparently converted to Christianity, though he put off baptism until the final year of his life in 337. While the sincerity of Constantine's conversion continues to be debated[62]—a question beyond the scope of the present study—how did Constantine's conversion affect Christianity in the Roman Empire both in the short-term and the long-term?

After tolerating Christianity in 312, Constantine gave the movement favored status in 324 upon defeating Licenius in battle and taking complete control of the empire. Some of the benefits extended to the church included clergy gaining tax exempt status, churches receiving funding, and government-sponsored construction of new church buildings. Though Christians had already been meeting for worship on Sunday, Constantine facilitated this practice by closing the markets officially making it a day of worship.[63] Christians began to occupy important roles in government and society and bishops were also given prominent status. Finally, the emperor was clearly concerned about unity within the church and got involved in the Donatist and Arian controversies, gathering the bishops involved and

60. Justin, *First Apology* 5–6, 65–67.

61. Eusebius, *Life of Constantine* 1.28–31; *Church History* 9.9; Lactantius, *On the Manner* 44.

62. Cf. Thompson, "From Sinner to Saint? Seeking a Consistent Constantine."

63. Eusebius, *Life of Constantine* 4.18.1.

sponsoring theological reflection toward the issues being resolved.[64] While the Council of Arles met in 314 to address the Donatist schism, the most famous gathering of bishops initiated by the emperor was the Council of Nicaea of 325. Interpreting Constantine's rise to power and the favor given to the church as a sign of divine triumph, Eusebius celebrated "one God, one Word and Savior, one emperor."[65]

Figure 1: Mosaic floor of Sufetula (Sbeitla, Tunisia) baptistery showing the post-Consantinian *chi-rho* symbol (copyright © Marcus Brooks; used with permission).

Irvin and Sunquist helpfully assert that "in a few short years, Christianity in the Mediterranean world went from being an illegal religion to the official creed of the Roman emperor."[66] They add, "Constantine's embrace of Christianity in the fourth century was the first step toward a great synthesis of religion, state, and culture in the Roman world."[67] Though Constantine's name is most often attached to the national religion or later state church paradigm—the "Constantinian church"—the emperor was surely not the

64. Hastings, *World History of Christianity*, 40.

65. Cited in ibid., 38,

66. Irvin and Sunquist, *History of the World Christian Movement*, 155.

67. Ibid.

sole player in this broader development. As noted, outside of Rome, King Tiridates of Armenia had already declared his country a Christian nation following his conversion and baptism in 301. It should also be remembered that Christianity was not made the official religion of the empire until the Emperor Theodosius' legislation in 380.[68] Yet, Constantine's alleged conversion certainly set into motion a pattern in which kings converted and then directed or at least influenced their subjects to do the same.[69]

The Constantinian paradigm not only shaped church and state relations for centuries to come but it also influenced how the church began to understand and practice Christian mission. As gospel expansion became synonymous with Christendom, it followed that compulsion and even violence were at times regarded as acceptable "missionary" methods. This development can be closely observed in Charlemagne's campaign against the Saxons in which he declared these personal enemies to be the church's enemies and they were given the opportunity to convert or face violence.[70] Robert comments, "The dark side of the growing power of Christendom was the increasing willingness of popes and kings to use force against groups that refused to accept the Catholic faith."[71] Newbigin adds, "It is easy to see with hindsight how quickly the church fell into the temptation of worldly power. It is easy to point . . . to the glaring contradiction between the Jesus of the Gospels and his followers occupying seats of power and wealth."[72]

The Constantinian phenomenon should not be simplistically regarded as a triumph of the church toward an automatic Christianization of the Roman Empire and other regions that accepted Christianity. Indeed, in the decades and centuries following Constantine's conversion, the narrative of the church and Christian mission remains complicated; however, in no way did it signal the end of Christian mission.[73] While Clovis and Charlemagne certainly forced Christianity on their subjects, missionaries such as Patrick, Augustine of Canterbury, and the Celtic monks seemingly worked within this paradigm and preached the gospel to a region or nation after first evangelizing its monarchs. Though Boniface's (680–754) eighth-century

68. Ibid., 113, 182–83.

69. Ibid., 238.

70. Bosch, *Transforming Mission*, 221.

71. Robert, *Christian Mission*, 24.

72. Newbigin, *Foolishness to the Greeks*, 100.

73. Cf. Ibid.; and Bosch, *Transforming Mission*, 237.

mission to the Frisians was certainly dependent on the political protection of the Frankish King Charles Martel, this arrangement was still not enough to save Boniface and his companions from martyrdom. Finally, it is quite ironic that monastic movements, which were clearly fueled in the fourth century by an anti-Constantinian spirit, also produced the greatest number of transcultural missionaries from the sixth century onward. In short, Christian mission continued in varying forms in the post-Constantine period, including during the Vandal conquest of Rome (ca. 409–493) and through the Byzantine resurgence (ca. 527–565).[74]

The Rise of Islam

Irvin and Sunquist write, "Within a century of the death of Muhammad, as many as half of the world's Christians were under Muslim political rule."[75] Just two years after Muhammad's death in 634, Khalid ibn Walid defeated a Byzantine army in battle in Damascus resulting in Syria coming under Arab-Muslim control a few years later. The Arabs gained control of Egypt by 640 and had conquered all of Persia by 642. By 670, the Arab conquest extended from Constantinople in the East to the Atlantic shores of Morocco in the West and by 700, after having defeated the last Byzantine armies, the Arabs controlled all of North Africa. An expanding empire with a religion at its center, the Arabs seemed quite adept at organizing and assimilating its conquered peoples and territories. The Muslim armies generally offered three possibilities to its conquered foes—conversion to Islam, *dhimmi* status, or jihad.

While many Christians did convert to Islam under the leadership rightly guided caliphs of Medina (632–661) and during the Ummayad Dynasty (661–750) that was based in Damascus, others accepted this *dhimmi* status. That is, in exchange for paying a tax, they were given protection and freedom to continue worshipping as Christians. Though Christian missions diminished greatly in Muslim lands during this period, there will still be some accounts of Christian–Muslim engagement that will be worth noting.

---

74. For further discussion, see Smither, "Did the Rise of Constantine Mean the End of Christian Mission?"

75. Irvin and Sunquist, *History of the World Christian Movement,* 271.

Egyptian Christians, Modern *Dhimmis*

Though the Muslim caliphate (an official ruling dynasty) ceased to exist with the demise of the Ottoman Empire nearly a century ago, the countries of the Arab world remain predominantly Muslim and their societies and governments are, of course, influenced by an Islamic worldview. As a result, it is not unusual for Christian minorities in the Middle East (modern *dhimmis*) to face discrimination and even encounter violence at times. Though Christians may number as high as 10 percent of Egypt's population of 80 million, the Pew Research Center indicated in 2011 that those numbers were actually difficult to confirm because of the oppressed status of Christians: "Egypt has very high government restrictions on religion as well as high social hostilities involving religion. (Most recently, a bombing outside a church in Alexandria during a New Year's Eve Mass killed 23 people and wounded more than 90.) These factors may lead some Christians, particularly converts from Islam, to be cautious about revealing their identity."[76]

Under these circumstances, how do Egyptian Christians worship and live out their faith? How do they approach Christian mission?

Frontiers of Thought

The gospel not only spread across geographical and cultural boundaries in varied social and political contexts in the first eight centuries, but the movement also encountered a worldview matrix that included a variety of philosophies and religions. Though space does not allow for a thorough discussion, let us briefly describe the major worldview systems that the church encountered.

Within the second and third centuries in particular, Gnosticism posed many challenges to Christian thought. Though scholars today struggle to formulate a comprehensive definition for the philosophy,[77] generally, Gnosticism viewed creation and matter in a negative light and taught that redemption came through a secret knowledge (*gnosis*) that liberated the spirit from the body. Irenaeus and Tertullian regarded the movement as a threat to the purity of the gospel and both men spilled much ink in articulating apologetics against Gnosticism. On the other hand, Clement of Alexandria forged his theology to some extent by appropriating Gnostic vocabulary.

As noted, the key reason that Christians were persecuted in the pre-Constantine period was on account of their impiety—the rejection

---

76. "Pew Research Center: Publications," February 16, 2011.

77. See Carl Smith, "Post-Bauer Scholarship on Gnosticism(s)."

of Roman paganism. As Roman religion was syncretistic and included Persian, Egyptian, and Phoenician deities in its pantheon, while also venerating the Roman emperor, the exclusive claims of Christianity were certainly repulsive to the imperial cult.[78] While the testimonies of the Scillitan martyrs, Perpetua and Felicitas, and Cyprian reveal a Christian rejection of paganism, Augustine's work *The City of God* serves as the most thorough Christian apologetic against it.

Outside of the Roman Empire, Persian Christians were also embracing the gospel in the context of another national religion, Zoroastrianism. A dualistic cult that emphasized a cosmic battle between light and darkness, Zoroastrian leaders also persecuted Christians for rejecting the national faith.[79]

Manicheanism, traditionally regarded as mix of Gnostic, Zoroastrianism, and neo-Platonic thought, and greatly concerned with the problem of evil, had followers from North Africa to China.[80] As many of its leaders were ascetic-type intellectuals, Manicheanism appealed to young thinkers such as Augustine who were disillusioned with the church. On the other hand, once Augustine came to faith, his first apologetic efforts—both in the form of public debates and treatises—were directed toward this sect that he had frequented for about a decade.

Finally, the Christian movement also interacted with adherents of the other monotheistic traditions—Judaism and Islam—in the period of our study. Though the church's posture toward the Jews was hardly missional in the patristic period, there were some exceptions such as Justin's dialogue with Trypho in Ephesus in the second century. While the expanding Arab-Muslim Empire quickly took control of Christian areas in the seventh and eighth centuries and there were many Christians that converted, there were still some *dhimmis* that engaged Muslims with the gospel.

As early Christian missionaries communicated the gospel to those with different worldviews outside of the church, there was also a type of mission field within the church as church leaders battled to preserve orthodoxy. One of the great points of contention was over correctly articulating the doctrine of Christ. In the first three centuries, the church responded to the heresy of Docetism—that Jesus was a mere phantom and only appeared

---

78. Wilken, *The Christians as the Romans Saw Them*, 48–67; cf. Kalantzis, *Caesar and the Lamb*, 16–18.

79. Moffet, *History of Christianity in Asia*, 1:106–12.

80. Coyle, "Mani, Manicheism," 520–25.

(*dokeo*) to have a human body.[81] Later controversies included adoptionism (Jesus being adopted as the Son of God and taking on divinity at his baptism)[82] and subordinationism (that Jesus was less than the Father). In the fourth century, Apollinarius (ca. 310–ca. 390) emphasized Jesus' divinity to such an extent that he essentially denied the Lord's human will and nature.[83] Finally, in the midst of a confusing theological battle with Cyril of Alexandria (ca. 376–444), Nestorius (ca. 386–ca. 451) seemed to teach that there were two Jesuses—a divine Jesus and a human one. Nestorius' Christology was largely responded to at the Council of Chalcedon of 451—a meeting that did much to alienate Greek speaking Christianity from the churches of Syria, Ethiopia, and the greater East. Most scholars today are reluctant to conclude that all Nestorian Christians—a term that became synonymous with eastern Christians—were heretical in their doctrine.[84]

Adoptionist and subordinationist thinking continued as the fourth-century fathers sought to understand and articulate how the Father, Son and Holy Spirit—particularly the Father and the Son—related together in essence and action. The Alexandrian Presbyter Arius (ca. 250–336), of course, taught that as the Father was eternal and uncreated and that the Son was created by the Father, then Jesus was necessarily subordinate to the Father. Though the issue was addressed at Nicaea in 325 and Arius was initially deposed, the Arian controversy raged on for most of the fourth century between three parties: the homoousions, who believed that the Father and the Son share the same essence; the homoeans, who asserted that the two have similar essence; and, to a lesser extent the anomeans, who saw the Father and Son as entirely different.[85] While this controversy was largely an issue within the church, there were Arian missionaries such as the homoean Ulfilas, who was set apart as a missionary-bishop to the Goths.

Also in the fourth and fifth centuries, the church wrestled with the doctrines of grace—including free will, the effects of the fall, and original sin—through the Pelagian controversy. Pelagius' (ca. 354–ca. 420/440) assertions that man did not have a sinful nature and that perfection was possible and even obligatory were answered quite thoroughly by Augustine in

81. Sweet, "Docetism," 24–31.

82. Muers, "Adoptionism," 50–58.

83. Kelly, *Early Christian Doctrines*, 289–301.

84. Irvin and Sunquist, *History of the World Christian Movement*, 281; also Ward, "Africa," 194–96.

85. Kelly, *Early Christian Doctrines*, 223–79.

a number of books and letters as well as through the Councils of Carthage (412), Milevus (416), and Carthage (418).[86] Finally, Augustine engaged another group—the Donatists—for instigating schism to the church in Africa in the fourth and fifth centuries. Though most commentators today would not regard them as a heretical group, Augustine considered the Donatists to be heretics for bringing disunity to the church and they became, in a sense, his mission field.[87]

Conclusion

It is difficult to understand any movement in history without some consideration of the context. The aim of this chapter has been to paint a picture of the backgrounds of mission in the early church. In broad strokes, the geographical expansion of the gospel has been considered as well as the political, social, and ideological contexts in which it spread. Building from this background and foundation, in the following chapters we will explore the personalities, strategies, and missiology of early Christian mission.

Questions for Reflection

1. Read Acts 2:5–12:

   Now there were dwelling in Jerusalem Jews, devout men from every nation under heaven. And at this sound the multitude came together, and they were bewildered, because each one was hearing them speak in his own language. And they were amazed and astonished, saying, "Are not all these who are speaking Galileans? And how is it that we hear, each of us in his own native language? Parthians and Medes and Elamites and residents of Mesopotamia, Judea and Cappadocia, Pontus and Asia, Phrygia and Pamphylia, Egypt and the parts of Libya belonging to Cyrene, and visitors from Rome, both Jews and proselytes, Cretans and Arabians—we hear them telling in our own tongues the mighty works of God." And all were amazed and perplexed, saying to one another, "What does this mean?"

2. Can a connection be made between these Jewish pilgrims who heard the gospel at Pentecost and the subsequent spread of Christianity to their homelands in the decades and centuries that followed?

---

86. Ibid., 357–74.
87. Cf. Smither, "Augustine, a Missionary to Heretics?"

3. In light of the gospel's spread across geographical and cultural boundaries in the first four centuries, how do we summarize the identity of early Christianity (i.e., was it a "western" faith)?

4. In light of the Arian Ulfilas' mission to the Goths, how important is theology to mission?

5. What are the dangers of the Constantinian paradigm for Christian mission? How might modern evangelicals be in danger of inappropriately using money and power in the practice of mission?

2

Who Were the Missionaries?

AFTER A RECEIVING A FINE education at Cambridge and also setting records in cricket, C. T. Studd (1860–1931) relinquished a sizeable inheri-
tance and spent his life serving as a missionary in China, India, and Central
Africa.[1] Around the same period, Mary Slessor (1848–1915), who grew up
in poverty in Scotland, ventured to Nigeria where, as a single woman, she
engaged in pioneer mission work.[2] In 1984, Mexican missionary Pablo Car-
illo founded Muslim People's International (PMI), the first Latin American missions agency focusing on the Muslim world. With sending bases
in Spain, Argentina, Brazil, and the United States, PMI currently has 120
laborers involved in mission work in many countries in the Muslim world.[3]

One of the highlights of studying the history of Christian missions is
encountering courageous people, often from very different backgrounds,
who stepped out in faith to cross land, sea, and culture, in order to proclaim the gospel. In this chapter, we want to pose the simple question, who
were the missionaries in the early church? While acknowledging that they
came from diverse geographical and cultural backgrounds, let us examine
some representative profiles of intercultural workers from 100 to 750. In
our study, we will meet official, full-time missionaries as well as those who
were involved in missions while pursuing other primary vocations. Finally,

1. Tucker, *From Jerusalem to Irian Jaya*, 314–19.

2. Ibid., 170–71.

3. Miller, "Mission-Minded Latinos," 70; also *PMI USA* (web site) http://www.pmi-
usa.org.

the argument will be made that many everyday Christians were also committed to mission.

Full-Time Missionaries

Though Alan Kreider has asserted that "the earliest Christians did not engage in public preaching; it was too dangerous,"[4] there does seem to be evidence for official, full-time evangelists who proclaimed the gospel publicly in the early church. While my aim is not to quibble over what constituted a public or private space, the point is that the mission and proclamation of early Christians was a known thing.[5]

Early church tradition suggests that some of the apostles and followers of the Lord also became full-time missionaries.[6] Though unable to provide firm historical support, the church in Armenia regards Thaddeus and Bartholomew as its founding evangelists.[7] On the other hand, the modern Coptic Church in Egypt—supported by the claims of Clement of Alexandria, Eusebius of Caesarea (ca. 260–341), and Jerome (347–420)—looks to the Gospel writer John Mark as its first missionary.[8] The most famous apostle-missionary account in early Christianity involves Thomas and his alleged mission to India. Unfortunately, the key literary evidence pointing to the mission is the third-century apocryphal work the *Acts of Thomas,* which tells a rather fanciful tale of Thomas going to prison after building a spiritual palace for a certain King Gundaphar.[9] Despite the credibility issues with the *Acts of Thomas,* other evidence actually offers some support for Thomas' work.[10] These include the discovery of first- to third-century Roman coins in southern India—an indication of significant trade between

4. Kreider, "They Alone Know the Right Way to Live," 169.

5. Green, *Evangelism in the Early Church,* 234–42.

6. Eusebius, *Church History* 3.1.1; *Acts of Thomas* 1.1; also Green, *Evangelism in the Early Church,* 235; and Moffett, *History of Christianity in Asia,* 1:26.

7. *The Armenian Church,* online: http://www.armenianchurch-ed.net/our-church/history-of-the-church/history/.

8. Eusebius, *Church History* 2.16; Jerome, *Lives of Illustrious Men* 36; also Oden, *How Africa Shaped the Christian Mind,* 18, 97, 125, 158–59, 194; and Oden, *The African Memory of Mark.*

9. A helpful excerpt can be found in Ehrman, *After the New Testament,* 13–17; also Neill, *History of Christian Missions,* 44–45; and Moffett, *History of Christianity in Asia,* 1:26–29.

10. Frykenberg, "India," 148–52.

India and the Roman Empire—and archaeological evidence confirming that King Gundaphar actually lived.[11] The fact also remains that when the Portuguese reached India in 1500, they encountered a community of 100,000 Christians in southern India, who through their oral history traced their spiritual lineage to the doubting apostle.[12]

Aside from these allusions to missions from the apostolic age, there is further evidence in the early church for full-time missionaries. Let us first consider the *Didache*, a late first-century or early second-century text that served as a discipleship manual for Gentile Christians. The fact that this work existed at all indicates that the gospel was crossing cultural boundaries as Gentiles in the ethnically diverse Roman Empire were embracing Christ. In the work, the anonymous author refers to a group of prophet-like evangelists who served as itinerant preachers. He writes: "Whosoever then comes and teaches you all these things aforesaid, receive him . . . Let everyone who 'comes in the name of the Lord' be received; but when you have tested him, you shall know him, for you shall have understanding of true and false. If who comes is a traveler, help him as much as you can, but he shall not remain with you more than two days, or, if need be, three."[13] While the readers were warned about being exploited by some questionable wandering prophets, the evidence still suggests that itinerant, cross-cultural ministry was happening during this period.

Similarly Eusebius of Caesarea, recounting the work of missionaries from the apostolic period to the fourth century, wrote:

> And there were many others besides these who were known in those days, and who occupied the first place among the successors of the apostles. And they also, being illustrious disciples of such great men, built up the foundations of the churches which had been laid by the apostles in every place, and preached the gospel more and more widely and scattered the saving seeds of the kingdom of heaven far and near throughout the whole world. For indeed most of the disciples of that time, animated by the divine word with a more ardent love for philosophy, had already fulfilled the command of the Savior, and had distributed their goods to the needy. Then starting out upon long journeys they performed the

11. Moffett, *History of Christianity in Asia,* 1:29–33.

12. Neill, *History of Christian Missions,* 122; also Moffett, *History of Christianity in Asia,* 1.33–36. Further evidence of Christian expansion into India from Persia has been discussed in Irvin and Sunquist, *History of the World Christian Movement,* 113–14.

13. *Didache* 11–13, cited in Schnabel, *Early Christian Mission,* 2:1527.

FULL TIME

office of evangelists, being filled with the desire to preach Christ to those who had not yet heard the word of faith, and to deliver to them the divine Gospels. And when they had only laid the foundations of the faith in foreign places, they appointed others as pastors, and entrusted them with the nurture of those that had recently been brought in, while they themselves went on again to other countries and nations, with the grace and the co-operation of God. For a great many wonderful works were done through them by the power of the divine Spirit, so that at the first hearing whole multitudes of men eagerly embraced the religion of the Creator of the universe.[14]

Hence, Eusebius also affirmed the work of missionaries, whose significant travels certainly led them to cross cultural boundaries, and he also highlights their role in establishing churches.

Finally, in the third century, Origen also made reference to full-time, traveling evangelists: "Some of them, accordingly, have made it their business to itinerate not only through cities, but even villages and country houses, that they might make converts to God. And no one would maintain that they did this for the sake of gain, when sometimes they would not accept even necessary sustenance."[15] In the context of his defense of Christianity against the pagan Celsus, Origen argues that these missionaries were known for their pure motives and that they were even deprived of basic provisions for the sake of the gospel.

Bivocational Missionaries

Though the evidence presented has shown that there were full-time missionaries in the early church, many others were also involved in intercultural mission work, though it was not their primary vocation. They most notably included bishops, teachers, philosophers, and monks.

Bishops. Some bishops—those set apart to pastor established churches—were quite known for their evangelistic and mission efforts. It should be noted that in the early church, the bishop generally emerged as a church organizer after a community had been evangelized and some semblance of a church had been planted.[16] Bruce affirms that "it was not until there

14. Eusebius, *Church History* 3.37.1–3.

15. Origen, *Against Celsus*, 3.9, cited in Schnabel, *Early Christian Mission*, 2.1528.

16. Irvin and Sunquist, *History of the World Christian Movement*, 237.

was a Christian community of reasonable dimensions in any place that a bishop was appointed to superintend them, and even then the normal practice was for the community in question to ask for a bishop."[17] While the work of a bishop was certainly a full-time job—Augustine even called it a "burden"—some bishops also took on the extra burden of cross-cultural mission work.[18]

Figure 2: Baptistery in the church at Hippo Regius (Annaba, Algeria).

In the second century, Ignatius of Antioch (d. 110) exhorted his fellow bishop Polycarp to "press on in your course and exhort all men that they may be saved."[19] Ignatius' letter to Polycarp was quite missional in its orientation and was part of a corpus of letters that the bishop wrote as he was being transported by Roman guard from his home in Asia toward martyrdom in Rome. Polycarp later followed suite and witnessed to Christ through his

17. Bruce, *Spreading Flame,* 398.

18. Smither, *Augustine as Mentor,* 126–27; also Bevans and Schroeder, *Constants in Context,* 119.

19. Ignatius, *Polycarp* 1, cited in Green, *Evangelism in the Early Church,* 239.

own execution by the Romans in Asia Minor. Hence, both men ministered and suffered in a diverse, multi-cultural environment.

Bishop Irenaeus of Lyons, originally from Greek-speaking Asia Minor, labored as a missionary-bishop in Gaul, which was a largely Latin-speaking region. Known for defending the church against Gnosticism—in part through becoming an expert in Gnostic thought—Irenaeus also made it a point to learn the local dialect of southern Gaul in order to preach in the pagan villages around Lyons.[20] Because of his commitment to minister in the heart languages of his host people, Irenaeus reported later in life that his command of his native Greek began to suffer as a result.[21]

After converting to Christianity through the witness of Origen in Palestinian Caesarea, Gregory Thaumaturgus returned home to Asia Minor where he intended to pursue a monastic lifestyle. In 240, he was ordained *in absentia* to be the bishop of the church of Neo-Caesarea in Pontus. Though this development was contrary to his plans, he did faithfully serve as the bishop and is remembered for evangelizing Pontus. Gregory's mission strategy was quite diverse. On one hand, he appealed to pagan intellectuals through his command of philosophy, mathematics, and law; on the other, he reached others through healing, exorcising demons, and preaching Scripture. His mission work was apparently so significant that Basil of Caesarea (ca. 329–ca. 379) made the hyperbolic claim that when Gregory arrived in Pontus there were only seventeen Christians; yet when he died, there were only seventeen pagans.[22]

Martin of Tours (ca. 316–397) was an important missionary-bishop of the fourth century. Originally from the Roman province of Pannonia (modern Hungary), Martin was dramatically converted to Christ while serving as a soldier in the Roman army. Following his conversion, he became a monk and established monasteries in Milan and Gaul, and on the island of Gallinaria (Italy). In 372, Martin was rather forcibly ordained as the bishop of Tours (Gaul) and like a number of other fourth-century bishops, including Basil and Augustine, he combined the vocations of monk and bishop. From this position, he labored to evangelize the pagan populations of Gaul through confronting pagan practices, destroying pagan temples,

20. Minns, "Irenaeus," 36–39.

21. Irenaeus, *Against All Heresies* 1.1; also Green, *Evangelism in the Early Church*, 240.

22. Basil, *On the Holy Spirit* 74; Basil, *Letter* 28; also Green, *Evangelism in the Early Church*, 268. I am indebted to my former student Joseph Super for his helpful research on Gregory, which has informed my thoughts here.

performing healings and other miracles, and demonstrating a holy life. In one sense, Martin's mission field was also within the church as he, along with his mentor Hilary of Poitiers (ca. 315–ca. 367), endeavored to defend the church in Gaul against the Arian heresy.

Table 1: **Early Christian Missionaries**

Missionary	Dates	Primary Role	Place of Service	Mission Methods
Ignatius of Antioch	d. 110	Bishop	Between Antioch and Rome	Preaching; writing; martyrdom
Polycarp of Smyrna	d. 156	Bishop	Asia	Preaching; martyrdom
Justin Martyr	ca. 100–165	Philosopher, teacher	Rome, Ephesus	Public debate; writing; martyrdom
Irenaeus of Lyons	ca. 115–200	Bishop	Gaul; Rome	Apologetics; preaching
Pantaenus	d. 200	Teacher	Alexandria; India	Teaching
Origen	ca. 185–254	Teacher	Alexandria; Palestine	Teaching; writing
Gregory Thaumaturgus	ca. 213–270	Bishop	Pontus; Asia Minor	Preaching; apologetics; healing; miracles; exorcism
Martin of Tours	ca. 316–397	Monk; bishop	Gaul	Preaching; apologetics; polemics; healings; miracles; establishing monasteries
Patrick of Ireland	ca. 387–ca. 461	Bishop	Ireland	Reaching local leaders; preaching; establishing churches
Columba	521–597	Monk	Scotland	Reaching local leaders; preaching; establishing monasteries

Missionary	Dates	Primary Role	Place of Service	Mission Methods
Gregory of Rome	540–604	Bishop	England	Sending missionaries
Augustine of Canterbury	d. 604	Monk; bishop	England	Reaching leaders; preaching; miracles; establishing monasteries; establishing churches
Columban	543–615	Monk	France; Italy	Reaching leaders; preaching; establishing monasteries
Boniface	680–754	Monk	Germany	Reaching leaders; preaching; confronting pagan religion; establishing monasteries; establishing churches; martyrdom
Nestorians	ca. 600–ca. 800	Monks; merchants	Central Asia; China	Reaching leaders; preaching; translating Scripture and literature; establishing monasteries; establishing churches

Despite the many legends associated with his life, Patrick of Ireland was a fifth-century bishop with a clear burden for missions. Ethnically British or perhaps even Welsh, Patrick was captured and enslaved by the Irish as a youth.[23] After escaping to Gaul, Patrick writes that he was compelled by a vision to return to Ireland as a missionary.[24] Possibly as early as 432, Patrick was set apart as a bishop for Ireland and served there until his death in 461. Throughout his *Confessions,* he describes himself as a stranger ministering at the "ends of the earth."[25] With an emphasis on reaching Irish pagans, Patrick's mission methods included seeking the favor of local leaders

23. O'Loughlin, *Saint Patrick,* 21; also Bruce, *Spreading Flame,* 373; and Thomas, *Christianity in Roman Britain,* 307.

24. Bruce, *Spreading Flame,* 374; also Thomas, *Christianity in Roman Britain,* 307–8.

25. O'Loughlin, *Saint Patrick,* 36–40; also Latourette, *History of the Expansion of Christianity,* 1:219.

and gaining permission to preach. Though he was surely not the first missionary to Ireland, Patrick was certainly a catalyst for Irish missions and by the mid- to late-fifth century, some 200 churches with around 100,000 reported converts had been established.[26]

A final missionary-bishop worth noting is Gregory of Rome (540–604). While Gregory was not personally involved in mission work, his contribution was noteworthy because he had a passion for sending missionaries. Venerable Bede (ca. 672–732), in his *Ecclesiastical History of the English People,* records that while Gregory sent out a number of missionaries, he had a particular burden for the Anglo people of Britain. After encountering English slave boys for sale in Rome, Gregory, in a play on words, declared that the "Anglos" (*angli*) should become "angels" (*angeli*).[27] Though some have questioned the veracity of this account, Gregory's compassion for the English became evident when he sent Augustine of Canterbury and a team of forty monks to evangelize them in 596.[28] The Roman bishop contributed to the English mission mostly by encouraging the band of monks to press on when they encountered hardship.[29] He also wrote many letters to Augustine offering practical ministry advice in the early stages of the mission.[30] Finally, Bede notes that Gregory's model for ministry continued to influence mission work in the British Isles in the generations after his death.[31]

Pastors and Missions

Though Gregory of Rome did not serve as a missionary himself, he was a pastor who had a vision for missions and labored to send out and support missionaries to unevangelized areas. In short, from his strategic role in the pastorate, he served as an advocate for missions. In recent years, one of the most compelling books on global missions, *Let the Nations Be Glad,* was authored by John Piper, who served for many years as the pastor of Bethlehem Baptist Church in Minneapolis, Minnesota. From his position as pastor, Piper has also overseen the sending of missionaries, supporting them financially, and offering them pastoral encouragement. In addition to his writing, Piper has been an

---

26. Tucker, *From Jerusalem to Irian Jaya,* 40; also Bruce, *Spreading Flame,* 375–83; and Robert, *Christian Mission,* 144–59.

27. Bede, *Ecclesiastical History* 2.1.

28. Ibid., 1.25.

29. Ibid., 1.23.

30. Ibid., 1.27, 30.

31. Ibid., 4.2

(continued)
outspoken advocate for making disciples of all nations—effectively calling the church in North America to think about the needs of the world and to be actively involved in evangelizing the least reached. Gregory and John Piper offer winsome models for how a local church pastor can take responsibility for the Great Commission, though his particular call may not be long-term ministry in another culture.

Philosophers. Aside from these bishops, some philosophers also functioned as bivocational missionaries. Justin Martyr, who originated from Palestine, set up a school in Rome and also spent time in Ephesus. Framing his Christian message in the vocabulary of Greek philosophy and communicating through written treatises and public debates, Justin's audience included the Jews, pagan intellectuals, and Christian heretics.[32] It is likely that he was executed after being condemned by a pagan opponent in Rome around 165.

Pantaenus, who is mostly known for directing the catechetical school of Alexandria, is also remembered for being a missionary to India. Eusebius writes:

> It is reported that Pantaenus was at that time especially conspicuous, as he had been educated in the philosophical system of those called Stoics. They say that he displayed such zeal for the divine word that he was appointed as a herald of the gospel of Christ to the nations in the East, and was sent as far as India. For indeed there were still many evangelists of the word who sought earnestly to use their inspired zeal, after the examples of the apostles, for the increase and building up of the divine word. Pantaenus was one of these, and is said to have gone to India . . . After many good deeds, Pantaenus finally became the head of the school at Alexandria, and expounded the treasures of divine doctrine both orally and in writing.[33]

Though details on Pantaenus' mission are lacking, he was apparently sent by Bishop Demetrius of Alexandria to teach philosophy and the Scriptures in India. Later, he returned to the catechetical school in Egypt where he, of course, mentored Clement of Alexandria and Origen.[34]

32. Ferguson, *Church History,* 73.

33. Eusebius, *Church History* 5.1–4; also Jerome, *Lives of Illustrious Men* 36.

34. Moffett, *History of Christianity in Asia,* 1:36–39.

Not unlike his former teacher, Origen, who praised the work of full-time missionaries in *Against Celsus*, also functioned as a missionary-teacher in a cross-cultural context. After a number of years of leading the Alexandrian school and confronting the Gnostic heresies in Egypt, Origen migrated to Palestinian Caesarea where he established a school and taught theology and philosophy. One of Origen's most famous students was Gregory Thaumaturgus, who came to Palestine with the express purpose of studying philosophy with Origen. In eulogizing Origen's life, Gregory described Origen's teaching:

> And from the very first day of his receiving us . . . he studied by all means to associate us closely with him, contriving all kinds of arguments, and . . . bringing all his powers to bear on that object. With that intent he lauded the lovers of philosophy with large laudations and many noble utterances . . . he reprehended ignorance and all the ignorant . . . and we were pierced by his argumentation as with an arrow from the very first occasion of our hearing him (for he was possessed of a rare combination of a certain sweet grace and persuasiveness, along with a strange power of constraint).[35]

Showing how this teaching led to his conversion, Gregory added, "And thus, like some spark lighting upon our inmost soul, love was kindled and burst into flame within us—a love at once to the holy word, the most lovely object of all, who attracts all irresistibly toward Himself by His unutterable beauty, and to this man, His friend and advocate. And being most mightily smitten by this love, I was persuaded to give up all those objects or pursuits which seem to us befitting."[36] In short, Origen used philosophy to lead his students to faith in Christ—an approach that immediately impacted Palestine and, later, through Gregory's ministry, Asia Minor as well.

Monks. Finally, the most significant group of bivocational missionaries, beginning in the sixth century, were monks.[37] This assertion may seem surprising to many modern readers because monasticism is often regarded as a solitary vocation of prayer and asceticism that in the end only benefits the monk. Indeed, the anchoretic or hermetic school of monasticism, championed by Antony (ca. 251–ca. 356) and Evagrius of Pontus (345–

35. Gregory Thaumaturgus, *The Oration and Panegyric Addressed to Origen* 6 (ANF 6).

36. Ibid.

37. Robert, *Christian Mission*, 25–26; also Irvin and Sunquist, *History of the World Christian Movement*, 353.

399), did emphasize an isolated spiritual journey. However, the majority of monks in the history of the church have been coenobitic or communal in their monastic outlook. That is, following the examples of men such as Pachomius, Basil, and Augustine, they founded monasteries because community itself was regarded as a viable means of spiritual growth.[38]

One distinctive feature of monastic life for anchorites and coenobites was manual labor. This work—a form of spiritual discipline as well as a means of survival—included such tasks as weaving rope, gardening, farming, and copying books. While some fourth- and fifth-century monk-bishops performed their monastic labor through serving the church as ordained ministers, many monks from the sixth-century onward fulfilled theirs through preaching and mission work. Eventually, this practice led to the founding of a number of missionary monastic orders, including the Franciscans (1209), the Dominicans (1221), and the Jesuits (1540). Let us consider several examples of coenobitic, missionary-monks from the sixth, seventh, and eighth centuries.

The most famous Irish missionary-monk was Columba (521–597), who was dubbed the apostle of Scotland. Bede writes: "[In 565], there came from Ireland to Britain a priest and abbot named Columba, a true monk in life no less than habit; he came to Britain to preach the word of God to the kingdoms of the Northern Picts . . . Columba came to Britain when Bridius [Brute] . . . a most powerful king, had been ruling over them for over eight years. Columba turned them to the faith of Christ by his words and example and so received the island of Iona from them in order to establish a monastery there."[39] From this account, we learn that Columba's approach was to seek first the favor of King Brute, who was apparently converted to the gospel, and who allowed Columba and his monks to begin a monastery at Iona. While their daily activities included prayer, fasting, study, and manual labor, the monks also labored as evangelists among the Pict people of the Scottish highlands—an area that had been evangelized to some degree in the fourth and fifth centuries by Bishop Ninian (ca. 360–430).[40]

In 590, Columban (543–615) left the monastery in Bangor and established a community of monks at Luxeuil, France, where he served for twenty years. Though he initially found favor with the local king and was given the freedom to preach, he was later expelled by the king of Burgundy

38. Smither, *Augustine as Mentor,* 64–65; also Bruce, *Spreading Flame,* 345.

39. Bede, *Ecclesiastical History* 3.4 (all translations from McClure and Collins).

40. Bruce, *Spreading Flame,* 386–93; also Thomas, *Christianity in Roman Britain,* 275–94.

for preaching against the king's immorality. After leaving Luxeuil, he and his monks continued evangelizing other parts of France and northern Italy. Later, Columban's disciple Gall (ca. 550–ca. 646) founded a monastery in Switzerland.[41] While the monastery served as a mission base for the Irish monks, it was also became an environment for copying Scripture—including ornate pieces such as the Book of Kells—and other works of Christian and classical literature.

As noted, Augustine of Canterbury (d. 604) and a group of forty Benedictine monks were sent by Bishop Gregory of Rome to evangelize the English in 596.[42] Bede vividly describes their approach to ministry—an integration of monastic and missional living: "They began to imitate the way of life of the apostles and of the primitive church. They were constantly engaged in prayers, in vigils and fasts; they preached the word of life to as many as they could; they despised all worldly things as foreign to them; they accepted only the necessaries of life from those whom they taught; in all things they practiced what they preached."[43] Their strategy included making contact with King Ethelbert of Kent (ca. 560–ca. 616), who apparently embraced Christianity and allowed the monks to proclaim the gospel freely and to establish churches. In the first year of their work, they reported that 10,000 Anglos had been baptized.[44] Bede reported that the English were receptive to the monks' message because they were "attracted by the pure life of the saints and by their most precious promises, whose truth they confirmed by performing many miracles."[45] As the English church quickly expanded, Augustine was consecrated as bishop of Canterbury and continued in that role until his death.[46]

While monks were used in part to evangelize England, a group of English monks led by Boniface were instrumental in reaching Germany with the gospel in the eighth century. Set apart in 722 as a missionary-bishop for Germany, Boniface also sought to reach kings and leaders, who then convinced their subjects of the superiority of the gospel. Afterward,

---

41. Neill, *History of Christian Missions*, 62–63.

42. Bede, *Ecclesiastical History* 1.23; also Bevans and Schroeder, *Constants in Context*, 123.

43. Ibid., 1.26.

44. Neill, *History of Christian Missions*, 58–59.

45. Bede, *Ecclesiastical History* 1.26.

46. Ibid., 1.27; also Irvin and Sunquist, *History of the World Christian Movement*, 327–39.

Boniface and his monks baptized entire villages of people who had embraced the faith of their leaders.[47] Boniface is probably most famous for his manner of confronting German paganism. In 724, he cut down the sacred oak dedicated to Thor at Geismar. After he emerged from the encounter unharmed, many Germans believed in Boniface's God and chose to build a church building from the oak tree. Though he enjoyed the protection of the Frankish King Charles Martel, this help was not enough as Boniface and a group of fifty monks were killed by an angry pagan mob in 754.[48]

A final monastic mission group worth noting is the Nestorian movement. They were connected in name to the embattled bishop of Constantinople who was condemned for his Christological heresy at the Councils of Ephesus (431) and Chalcedon (451).[49] While recent research on Nestorius' (ca. 381–451) theology is challenging traditional regard for him, the Nestorian missions movement should not be automatically deemed heretical.[50] Following the rise of Islam in the seventh century, the Nestorian movement was the only expression of Christianity that had any life East of Antioch. With significant churches in Edessa, Nisibis, and Seleucia-Ctesiphon, the movement expanded along the trade routes between Arabia and Central Asia.[51] Over time, "Nestorian" and "Christian" became synonymous terms in Asia.

The most celebrated Nestorian missionary monk was Alopen, who reached China in 635. After finding favor with the Emperor T'ai Sung, the Nestorian monks were free to proclaim the "luminous religion of Syria" and to establish a church.[52] While their monastic lifestyles were apparently impressive in the Buddhist context, the Nestorians learned Chinese and translated some key works of Christian literature into the language.[53] Though the Nestorians endured several periods of persecution from the seventh to tenth century, and the movement seemed to disappear by 980,

---

47. Bevans and Schroeder, *Constants in Context*, 125–26.

48. Neill, *History of Christian Missions*, 64–67.

49. Nestorius stood accused of concluding that Jesus was two people—a divine Son of God and a human being. He was opposed by Cyril of Alexandria who emphasized the unity of a divine and human Jesus.

50. Moffett, *History of Christianity in Asia*, 1:175–80, 312.

51. Irvin and Sunquist, *History of the World Christian Movement*, 278.

52. Moffett, *History of Christianity in Asia*, 1:288.

53. Bevans and Schroeder, *Constants in Context*, 105.

there were probably as many as 3,000 Nestorian missionaries in China in the ninth century.[54]

Lay and Anonymous Missionaries

It seems natural that these bishops, philosophers, and monks—all students of Scripture and its related disciplines—would be spokespersons for the Christian faith. However, laymen—including businessmen and merchants, colonists, and soldiers—also played a significant role in early Christian mission. Though his intention was to mock the church, the pagan Celsus confirms that unsophisticated, uneducated Christian tradesmen were active in sharing the gospel.[55] Similarly, Justin's *First Apology* highlights the integrity of Christian businessmen in an otherwise dishonest marketplace.[56]

Such accounts reveal an important quality of lay mission in the early church—that Christians were integrated members of their communities. To be sure, the pre-Constantinian church in the Roman Empire experienced sporadic and varying degrees of discrimination and persecution from the greater pagan society and, at times, even from the imperial authorities. Branded as members of a new and illegitimate religion, the Christians were regarded as traitors in a Roman society that considered piety toward the traditional deities as the mark of a good citizen.[57] Though Christian communities characteristically met in homes during the pre-Constantinian era and others possibly gathered under the creative guise of a funerary association, we should not assume that Christians were segregated or marginalized from the greater society.[58] As noted, Pliny's observation about Christians in second-century Bithynia and Tertullian's claims about second- and third-century Carthage indicate otherwise. Decius, Valerian, and Diocletian's empire-wide persecutions against the church, which included purges of the Senate, confiscating property from the wealthy, and even arresting royal family members, also show that Christians were quite integrated into daily

---

54. Moffett, *History of Christianity in Asia,* 1:293–314; Neill, *History of Christian Missions,* 82–83.

55. Origen, *Against Celsus* 3.55; also Schnabel, *Early Christian Mission,* 2.1526.

56. Justin, *First Apology* 16; also Schnabel, *Early Christian Mission,* 2.1526.

57. See Fox, *Pagans and Christians,* 43, 66; Sordi, *The Christians and the Roman Empire,* 83, 125; and Frend, *Martyrdom and Persecution,* 106, 110.

58. This will be discussed further in chapter 8.

Roman life.[59] This evidence supports the view of the anonymous author of the second-century *Epistle to Diognetus* who wrote:

> For Christians are no different from other people in terms of their country, language or customs. Nowhere do they inhabit cities of their own, or live life out of the ordinary . . . They inhabit both Greek and barbarian cities according to the lot assigned to each . . . they participate in all things as citizens . . . They live in their respective countries, but only as resident aliens; they participate in all things as citizens, and they endure all things as foreigners. They marry like everyone else and have children, but they do not expose them once they are born. They share their meals but not their sexual partners. They are found in the flesh but do not live according to the flesh. They live on earth but participate in the life of heaven. [60]

In short, early Christians in the Roman Empire were "in the world but not of the world" and testified to their eternal hope from their temporal place in society.

Apparently, many laymen participated in a largely anonymous and otherwise volunteer missionary movement—one of the most remarkable qualities of early Christian mission. Harnack asserts that "the great mission of Christianity was in reality accomplished by means of informal missionaries."[61] Stephen Neill adds, "Every Christian was a witness . . . nothing is more notable than the anonymity of these early missionaries."[62] Indeed, it is not insignificant that the two largest communions in the early western church—Rome and Carthage—had undocumented origins.[63]

---

59. Sordi, *Christians and the Roman Empire*, 114; Eusebius, *Church History*, 8.1; also Kreider, "They Alone Known the Right Way to Live," 171. Valerian's edicts came in 257–258 while Diocletian's were given between 303–305.

60. *Epistle to Diognetus* 5.1–6, cited in Schnabel, *Early Christian Mission*, 2.1566.

61. Harnack, *Mission and Expansion of Christianity*, 368; also Hastings, *World History of Christianity*, 27.

62. Neill, *History of Christian Missions*, 24.

63. Schnabel, *Early Christian Mission*, 2:1492.

Work and Mission

The majority of missionaries in the early church did not consider missions to be their primary vocation; rather, in addition to their "day job" as bishops, monks, teachers, merchants, and other vocations, they were engaged in cross-cultural ministry. Today, an increasing number of Christian workers and missions organizations are rethinking the nineteenth- and twentieth- century "professional ministry model," which presumed that one could freely enter a country with a missionary identity. This paradigm shift is due in part to changing political climates in which conventional Christian mission efforts are no longer welcome; however, it is also due to missionaries beginning to value work (i.e., business, teaching, nursing) as forms of worship that glorify God and serve the unreached in a tangible way. These values can be observed through the efforts of Interserve, an organization that helps Christian professionals find jobs in the fields of medicine, business, and education, in order to minister the gospel in Word and deed.[64] Similarly, others are embracing a mission philosophy known as Business as Mission (BAM)—"the utilization of for-profit businesses as instruments for global mission."[65] Through running a business according to biblical principles, creating jobs, and bringing transformation to communities, the verbal witness of BAM practitioners is greatly supported by their excellent work in a community. Hence, the early church bivocational missionary model is probably more relevant for many global contexts today than the nineteenth- and twentieth-century model.

North African Christianity, in particular, provides an intriguing case study for anonymous mission work. Before Augustine made his mark in patristic theology in the fourth and fifth centuries and prior to Cyprian's innovation in organizing the Carthage church and providing oversight to the bishops during mid-third-century African church councils, the African church had already grown significantly. Though Tertullian's claim that Christians were the majority in Carthage is doubtful, the Council of Carthage of 220 presided over by Agrippinus and attended by seventy bishops from a single African province (Proconsular Africa) testifies to a developed African church by the early third century. It should be noted that the council of 220 occurred just forty years after the first literary reference to Christianity in Africa—the account of the martyrs of Scilli who were condemned at Carthage in 180. The fact that a majority of these twelve martyrs (seven

---

64. *Interserve International* online: http://www.interserve.org/.

65. Johnson and Rundle, "Distinctives and Challenges of Business as Mission," 25. For more recent discussions on BAM, see Tunehag et al., "Business as Mission"; Johnson, *Business as Mission;* and Rundle and Steffen, *Great Commission Companies.*

men and five women) had Punic-Berber names signifies that the church had penetrated the African interior, which provides further evidence that Christianity was present in North Africa well before 180. Also, the catacombs of Hadrumetum, which contain at least fifteen thousand graves of second- to fourth-century Christians, have mid-second-century origins.[66] Though Carthage was probably the first African city touched by the gospel, the French archaeologist Paul Monceaux discovered Christian graves in Jewish cemeteries in Cyrene, which date to the early second century.[67]

Hence, North African Christianity had early beginnings (at least early second-century or even late first-century) that were strikingly anonymous. Decret concludes: "The opening pages of North African Christianity seem to have no connection with the apostolic period. Nor is there a great episode of a golden legend, a great saint, or an apostle arriving on the African shores to convert the unbelievers. Rather this history opens through the testimonies of blood."[68] Hence, North Africa was probably first evangelized by Christian merchants, colonists, and even soldiers. Like the bishops, philosophers, monks, and others mentioned, the early African Christians were integrated into the daily life of their social context and seemed accustomed to witnessing freely about their Christian faith.[69]

Conclusion

What can we learn from these profiles of early Christian missionaries? First, the early church did take seriously the command of Jesus to make disciples of all nations. As the author of the *Didache*, Origen, and Eusebius recount, there were full-time, official missionaries who traveled and crossed cultures in order to proclaim the Gospel and to establish churches. Even the accounts of apostolic mission that lack historical credibility point to the church's concern for and involvement in mission. In short, the early church was a missionary church.

Second, while there were full-time missionaries, this seems to be the exception more than the norm. Rather, as we have shown, bishops, philosophers, and monks engaged in transcultural mission while continuing to serve in their primary vocations. They clearly showed a conviction for

66. Decret, *Early Christianity in North Africa*, 11–12.

67. Latourette, *History of the Expansion of Christianity*, 1:92.

68. Decret, *Early Christianity in North Africa*, 10.

69. Schnabel, *Early Christian Mission*, 2:1548.

obeying the Lord's command and effectively integrated missions into their everyday work.

Finally, while it is impressive that church leaders, teachers, and monks regarded mission work as a valuable part of their religious vocation, it is even more meaningful that everyday Christians were also convinced of the priority of mission. Our discussion of the anonymous missions movement in North Africa and the general observation that Christians were integrated into the daily life of the ancient world cultures strongly suggest that missions was not the work of a specialized group; rather, it was the responsibility of every Christian. The French historian Henri Irénée Marrou has helpfully concluded: "The whole church considered itself to be involved in mission and to have a missionary duty, and every believer was a witness, felt called to the work of evangelization, even so far as the supreme witness of bloody martyrdom that was always on the horizon. This is perhaps the greatest lesson that Christians today can receive from their oldest brothers in the faith."[70]

Questions for Reflection

1. Read 2 Thess 2:8–12:

   So, being affectionately desirous of you, we were ready to share with you not only the gospel of God but also our own selves, because you had become very dear to us. For you remember, brothers, our labor and toil: we worked night and day, that we might not be a burden to any of you, while we proclaimed to you the gospel of God. You are witnesses, and God also, how holy and righteous and blameless was our conduct toward you believers. For you know how, like a father with his children, we exhorted each one of you and encouraged you and charged you to walk in a manner worthy of God, who calls you into his own kingdom and glory.

   In Paul's ministry in Thessalonica, what was the relationship between his physical labor and his gospel witness?

2. What can today's ministers learn from the missions commitment of early bishops, philosophers, and monks? What is the responsibility of full-time pastors, youth pastors, and others toward global missions?

3. What can modern Christians learn from the example of early Christians who were integrally involved in their communities? How can Christians who are not full-time ministers serve as missionaries?

70. Cited in Blocher and Blandenier, *Evangelization of the World*, 40.

4. What can be learned from the lay missions movement of the early church? What alternatives are there to the "professional" missionary model (where one is fully supported to do missions and their identity is that of a missionary)?

5. A number of the missionaries discussed in this chapter first make contact with local authorities and gained permission to proclaim Christ? Is such a strategy relevant today in your context?

3

Suffering

In 1999, AN INTERNATIONAL GROUP of global mission leaders gathered at Iguassu Falls, Brazil for a consultation on global missiology. One outcome of the gathering was the publication of the "Iguassu Affirmation," which outlined some key values for moving forward in mission in the twenty-first century. After some initial declarations on the Lordship of Christ and the primacy of the gospel, declaration six addressed the reality of and response to suffering in the global church: "Suffering, persecution and martyrdom are present realities for many Christians. We acknowledge that our obedience in mission involves suffering and recognize that the church is experiencing this. We affirm our privilege and responsibility to pray for those undergoing persecution. We are called to share in their pain, do what we can to relieve their sufferings, and work for human rights and religious freedom."[1]

In the minds of these declaration writers, suffering is an inevitable part and consequence of making disciples of all nations. Though advocacy for suffering Christians is certainly advised, the affirmation does not make the alleviation of suffering its highest priority. Many early Christians would have also resonated with these thoughts. As we have shown, discrimination and even persecution against followers of Christ—those living within and outside of the Roman Empire—was not uncommon during our period of study.

1. "Iguassu Affirmation," 18.

In reality, the Christian movement was founded upon and birthed through suffering and persecution. As much as anything, the task of the Gospel writers was to recount the sufferings of Jesus, especially his death, burial, and resurrection. While the redemptive work at the cross was the basis for Christ's saving work on behalf of humanity, Mark remembers that Jesus' suffering directly led to the faith of a Roman centurion who declared, "Truly, this man was the Son of God."[2] In a letter to Corinthian believers, the Apostle Paul described rather vividly his own suffering while proclaiming the gospel: "Five times I received at the hands of the Jews the forty lashes less one. Three times I was beaten with rods. Once I was stoned. Three times I was shipwrecked; a night and a day I was adrift at sea; on frequent journeys, in danger from rivers, danger from robbers, danger from my own people, danger from Gentiles, danger in the city, danger in the wilderness, danger at sea, danger from false brothers; in toil and hardship, through many a sleepless night, in hunger and thirst, often without food, in cold and exposure."[3] Elsewhere, Paul summarized his journey of following Christ and suffering in mission by stating bluntly, "I bear on my body the marks of Jesus."[4] Commenting on John the Evangelist's perspective on suffering, especially in the book of Revelation, Flemming adds, "In the world in which John and his readers live, bearing witness to Jesus is a costly business . . . the result may be the shedding of the blood of the saints. John beholds in heaven 'the souls of those who had been slaughtered for the word of God and for the testimony they had given.' (Rev. 6:9)"[5]

As suffering was endured by Christ, his disciples, and Paul, it was also the expected reality of the growing church movement in the first few centuries and many church leaders, such as Ignatius of Antioch and Cyprian, who sought to imitate Christ in this way.[6] Fox adds, "The most excellent Christians in the early church were . . . the Christians whom pagans put to death. The spread of Christianity, the conversions, the overachievement took place in an era of persecution."[7]

While discrimination and other forms of persecution were quite normal for the early Christians, particularly in the pre-Constantine period,

2. Mark 15:39.

3. 2 Cor 11:24–27.

4. Gal 6:17.

5. Flemming, *Contextualization in the New Testament*, 281–82.

6. Fox, *Pagans and Christians*, 437; also Frend, *Martyrdom and Persecution*, 150–51.

7. Fox, *Pagans and Christians*, 419.

this reality did in some cases lead to excesses: confessors receiving an exalted, priestly type status; lapsed Christians seeking forgiveness through voluntary martyrdom; and the rise of a cult of martyrs. Though these developments cannot be ignored and they were certainly addressed by the church fathers in sermons, writings, and church councils, such excesses and even a resulting theology of martyrdom are beyond the aims of the present chapter and will not be discussed.[8]

Given the phenomenon of Christian suffering through the first four centuries, the aim of this chapter is to ask, how did suffering contribute to and influence Christian mission? Through examining various accounts of persecution and martyrdom, including the words and actions of those who suffered, we will be able to draw some conclusions and argue that, in an indirect manner, suffering did serve as a strategic means for the advancement of the gospel. Specifically, it will be shown that the public context of persecution allowed Christians the opportunity to witness verbally about their faith and to clarify and defend the gospel. In some cases, it was reported that some bystanders were converted to Christianity because of the persecution they witnessed, while in other cases, non-Christian observers sympathized with suffering Christians—an influence that seemed to lay further groundwork for the growth of the church. Persecution against Christians also resulted in apologetics, written treatises that defended and articulated Christian belief. Finally, suffering seemed to invigorate the church and its mission as martyrs were remembered on feast days, through sermons, sacred biographies (*vitae*) and even through the construction of churches.

---

8. For more discussion, see Fox, *Pagans and Christians,* 442–60; Frend, *Martyrdom and Persecution,* 254–84; and Ferguson, "Martyr, Martyrdom," 726–27.

**Figure 3: Mosaic depicting Daniel in the lions' den,
an inspiration to suffering North African Christians.**

A Verbal Witness

The word *martyr* (*martus*) literally means "a witness," while the verbal form (*martureō*) refers to the action of witnessing. In much of the New Testament, the term is used to describe eyewitnesses of Christ; however, in Revelation 2:13, John begins to use it to distinguish those that have witnessed unto Christ by giving their lives. According to Ferguson, this was how the word was commonly used by the church before the end of the second century.[9] During the most intense periods of persecution, many were executed for refusing to offer incense or sacrifices to the pagan gods or emperors. While ultimately testifying to Christ by laying down their lives, many believers were also recorded giving a verbal witness during their arrest and court

9. Ferguson, "Martyr, Martyrdom," 724; cf. Moss, *Ancient Christian Martyrdom*, 2–3.

proceedings. The following survey of the key martyrdom records—acts of the martyrs (*acta*) or martyrdoms (*passio*)—will reveal such testimony.[10]

On one level, this verbal witness included the simple confession of being a Christian. In the famous account of Polycarp of Smyra, the bishop defended his refusal to offer the pagan sacrifice by stating, "For eighty and six years I have been his servant, and he has done me no wrong, and how can I blaspheme my king who saved me?" Later in the same account, the prosecuting governor based his verdict on the fact that "Polycarp has confessed that he is a Christian."[11]

In the late second century in neighboring Pergamum (Asia Minor), Carpus responded to the order to sacrifice by stating, "I am a Christian . . . and I venerate Christ the Son of God . . . I will not sacrifice to such idols as these . . . May the gods be destroyed who have not made heaven and earth." His fellow martyr Papylus added, "I have served Christ from my youth and I have never offered sacrifice to idols. I am a Christian."[12]

In the well-known late second century account of the martyrs of Lyons, these Christians offered similar confessions of faith at different stages of their prosecution. After declaring he was a Christian, Vettius Epagathus was thrown into prison. Blandina, Biblis, and Sanctus managed to give a verbal witness while being tortured. In the case of Sanctus, his testimony was repeatedly heard by the pagan crowd.[13]

Similar confessions were recorded in the North African context from the late second to mid-third century. Speratus, one of the Scillitan martyrs, declared during his trial: "I do not recognize the empire of this world. Rather, I serve that God whom no man has seen, nor can see, with these eyes." During the course of the trial, each member individually confessed, "I am a Christian," which served as the concluding evidence for their condemnation.[14] Some twenty years later, Perpetua, when asked by the governor if she was a Christian simply replied, "Yes, I am." During her arrest and in-

10. Though the accounts of martyrdom are considered by some to be hagiography, a genre that is overly biased and historically unreliable, my preference in this discussion is to listen to how the church has remembered martyrdom and how martyrs were depicted witnessing to Christ. The most reliable manuscripts, collected and translated by Herbert Mursurillo (*Acts of the Christian Martyrs*), will be our primary source for evaluation.

11. *Martyrdom of Polycarp* 8, 9, 12. Unless otherwise noted, all English translations of these and other acts are from Mursurillo, *Acts of the Christian Martyrs*.

12. *Acts of Carpus, Papylus, and Agathonicê*.

13. *Martyrs of Lyons and Vienne* 1; Frend, *Martyrdom and Persecution*, 1–21.

14. *Acts of the Scillitan Martyrs*.

terrogation, she even had opportunities to communicate the gospel to her own father.[15] During his trial, exile, and eventual execution in Carthage, Cyprian testified to his faith and his role of being a Christian leader: "I am a Christian and a bishop. I recognize no other gods but the one true God who made heaven and earth, and the sea, and that that is in them."[16] Finally, in the case of James and Marian in neighboring Numidia, the narrator of their martyrdom remembered that as he was tortured James "deliberately confessed that he was not only a Christian but also that he was a deacon."[17]

During the Decian persecution, the Presbyter Pionius was arrested and ordered by the Roman officials of Smyrna to eat meat sacrificed to idols. When taken into the theatre where his trial became much more public, Pionius apparently saw this as an opportunity to convince his hearers of the truth of the gospel. Before being burned alive, he repeatedly confessed: "I am a Christian . . . [I worship] the God who is almighty . . . who made the heaven and the earth and all things that are in them."[18]

A number of martyrs went beyond this simple confession of faith and sought to clarify aspects of the gospel. Polycarp expressed eagerness to do this when he said to his interrogators: "if you would like to learn the doctrine of Christianity, set aside a day and listen."[19] Though not granted that much time, Justin responded to the Prefect Rusticus' queries about the nature of his faith by offering this defense: "I have committed myself to the true doctrines of the Christians . . . the belief that we piously hold regarding the God of the Christians, whom alone we hold to be the craftsman of the whole world from the beginning, and also regarding Jesus Christ, the child of God, who was foretold by the prophets as one who was to come down to mankind as a herald of salvation and teacher of good doctrines."[20]

In the late second century in Asia, Apollonius declared at his trial before the Prefect Perennis, "Yes, I am a Christian . . . and hence I worship and fear the God who made heaven and earth, the sea and all that is in them." After praying for the emperor and the welfare of the empire, Apollonius added that the gospel could only be grasped by believers—"the Lord's word is for the heart that can see, just as eyes can see the light." Prior to his

15. *Passion of Perpetua and Felicitas* 3, 5–6.

16. *Acts of Cyprian* 1, 3.

17. *Martyrdom of Marian and James* 5.

18. *Martyrdom of Pionius the Presbyter and his Companions* 7–9, 15–16.

19. *Martyrdom of Polycarp* 10.

20. *Acts of Justin and Companions* 2.

execution, he clarified the gospel further by delivering a short sermon—almost creedal in structure—on the person and work of Christ:

> Jesus Christ, he who was our Savior . . . became man in Judea; he was righteous in all things and was filled with divine wisdom. Lovingly did he teach us who was the God of all things, and what was the purpose of virtue in a life of holiness, adapting his words to the minds of men. By his passion he destroyed the roots of sin . . . to worship the immortal God alone, to believe that the soul is immortal, to be convinced that there will be a judgment after death, and that there will be a reward given by God after the resurrection.[21]

Similarly, during the Great Persecution under Diocletian, Julius, a veteran of the Roman army, refused to burn incense to the emperor and confessed before the prefect, "I am a Christian." In a rather concise manner, Julius communicated the person and work of Christ and then invited his hearers to believe: "It was he [Jesus] who died for our sins . . . in order to give us eternal life. This same man Christ is God and abides forever and ever. Whoever believes in him will have eternal life; and whoever denies him will have eternal punishment."[22]

Prison Discipleship

Wagdi Iskander grew up in a Muslim family and lived as a devout Muslim until he was converted to Christ through the prayers and patient witness of a friend at university. Once word of his conversion became public, he was arrested, imprisoned, and sentenced to death by hanging. According to Wagdi, each Friday a prisoner was taken and was executed publicly. Over the course of the weeks in prison, some mature Christians, also in prison for their faith, took time to disciple Wagdi and encourage him to stand strong for the Lord when it came time for him to die. Indeed, during this period, Wagdi watched some of these believers leave the prison and never return. On the Friday morning that Wagdi was to be hung, he was awakened to the sounds of shots being fired in the streets as a neighboring country had invaded. With the prison guards immediately drafted into the already small army, Wagdi and the other prisoners were allowed to go free. After escaping his country and eventually settling in Canada, Wagdi received theological training and became a pastor. Resembling some of the early Christian martyrs

---

21. *Martyrdom of the Saintly and Blessed Apostle Apollonius, also called Sakeas.*
22. *Martyrdom of Julius the Veteran,* 1–3; cf. Kalantzis, *Caesar and the Lamb,* 163–67.

> *(continued)*
> discussed in this chapter, Wagdi was mentored by other Christians and grew in his faith in the context of prison and awaiting execution.[23]

Though some chose to clarify aspects of the gospel, other martyrs preached a rather prophetic message to their captors. After being threatened with fire, Polycarp lashed back: "The fire you threaten me with burns merely for a time and is soon extinguished. It is clear you are ignorant of the fire of everlasting punishment and of the judgment that is to come."[24] Before being whipped and having spikes driven through his ankles, Conon, an elderly believer in Pamphylia, declared to the authorities: "How could you thus blaspheme against the God of all things when your breath is in his hands? . . . Do you think you can terrify me by threatening me with mere words and thus suppose you can change my mind? . . . Beware lest the Judge sentence you to a Hades that is unsurpassed, a fire unquenchable forever."[25] Finally, prior to their executions, Revocatus, Saturninus, and Secundulus—companions of Perpetua and Felicitas—warned the crowd gathered in the Carthage amphitheater of God's coming judgment.[26]

In summary, it seems that many of the early Christian confessors were quite aware of their opportunity and obligation to proclaim the gospel amid their suffering. These values are well illustrated through the prayers of Paul of Palestine as he was about to be put to death. Eusebius records: "After this he offered up prayer for our enemies, the Jews, many of whom at that time were standing around him: then he went on in his supplication, and prayed for the Samaritans, and for those among the Gentiles who were without knowledge; he prayed that they might be converted to the knowledge of the truth."[27]

---

23. Wagdi Iskander recounted his story to me personally in 1997.

24. *Martyrdom of Polycarp* 10.

25. *Martyrdom of Conon* 5.

26. *Passion of Perpetua and Felicitas* 18.

27. Eusebius, *History of the Martyrs in Palestine* 32–33 (all translations from NPNF 2:1).

Proclamation and Truth

In addition to these individual confessions of faith, statements that clarified the gospel, and even words of warning, some martyred Christians used
their forum of suffering to attest to the truth of the gospel. Apollonius stated
rather bluntly, "we do not find it hard to die for the true God."[28] In his work,
Exhortation to Martyrdom, Origen's central argument was that the Christian faith was ultimately true because people were willing to suffer for it.[29]
Justin made a similar argument in his *Second Apology* when he wrote: "no
one was persuaded by Socrates to die for this teaching of his. But they were
persuaded by Christ."[30] Parvis adds that for Justin, martyrdom was "simply
a consequence of knowing what mattered" because he was convinced that
the gospel was true.[31]

Standing firmly on the truth of the gospel, others also used this opportunity to challenge wrong belief, particularly that of the Jews, heretics,
and pagans. During his arrest, Pionius confronted his Jewish opponents in
Smyrna. In his polemics, he denied claims that Christians practiced sor-
cery, defended the doctrine of Jesus' resurrection, and then condemned the
Jews for their own unbelief in the Messiah.[32]

Ignatius used the occasion of his arrest to challenge heretical thinking.[33] Frend writes that for Ignatius, "Martyrdom . . . had yet another object,
namely, the vindication of the reality of Christ's earthly ministry."[34] He was,
of course, challenging the Docetic view that Christ did not have an authentic body or humanity. In his *Letter to the Trallians*, Ignatius argues: "But if
some atheists (that is unbelievers) say he only suffered in appearance only
(while they exist in appearance only!), why am I in chains? And why do I
want to fight with wild beasts? If that is the case, I die for no reason; what is
more, I am telling lies about the Lord."[35] Frend helpfully summarizes: "Here
was the first explicit association of martyrdom with orthodox Christology.

28. *Martyrdom of Apollonius.*

29. Frend, *Martyrdom and Persecution*, 288.

30. Justin, *Second Apology*, 10.8, cited in Parvis, "Justin Martyr," 12.

31. Parvis, "Justin Martyr," 13.

32. *Martyrdom of Pionius the Presbyter and his Companions*, 4, 13–14; Fox, *Pagans and Christians*, 480–81.

33. For more on the relationship between martyrdom and orthodoxy in Irenaeus and Eusebius of Caesarea, see Moss, *Ancient Christian Martyrdom*, 116–19.

34. Frend, *Martyrdom and Persecution*, 153.

35. Ignatius, *Letter to the Trallians* 10, cited in Holmes, *Apostolic Fathers*, 110–11.

To Ignatius, as to Justin and Irenaeus, it was impossible for one who did not accept the reality of the incarnation to die a blood witness to Christ. Neither Docetist nor Gnostic could be a man of martyrdom."[36]

Finally, a number of martyrs used the forum of suffering to confront pagan worship and practices—the predominant worldview of those persecuting the church. In Smyrna, Pionius and his companions encountered pagans who wanted to persuade the Christians to return to Roman worship. Interestingly, Pionius appealed to Socrates and other philosophers to show the futility of the pagan perspective.[37] During his imprisonment in Carthage, Montanus aimed his Christian witness in part at pagans—those who "worship statues or idols made by men."[38] While appearing before the Roman authorities in Spain, Eulogius was asked if he worshiped his Bishop Fructuosus—a question that was certainly framed from a pagan perspective. Eulogius replied clearly, "I do not worship Fructuosus, but I worship the one whom he worships."[39]

Perhaps the most interesting Christian witness against paganism was given by soldiers in the Roman army.[40] In one case, Maximilian, an African Christian, refused to enlist in the military at all—a decision that led to his execution—because his conscience would not allow him to perform the pagan rituals expected of soldiers.[41] Another African, Marcellus, suffered capital punishment for withdrawing from the army after declaring: "I am a soldier of Jesus Christ, the eternal king. From now I cease to serve your emperors and I despise the worship of your gods of wood and stone, for they are deaf and dumb images."[42] In Palestine, a soldier named Marinus was denounced for refusing to make sacrifices after becoming convinced that the teachings of Scripture did not allow for this.[43] Finally, Dasius met a similar fate for refusing to make a sacrifice during the pagan festival of Saturn. He offered this simple defense: "Seeing that you force me to such a

36. Frend, *Martyrdom and Persecution*, 153.

37. *Martyrdom of Pionius the Presbyter and his Companions* 4, 17.

38. *Martyrdom of Saints Montanus and Lucius* 14.

39. *Martyrdom of Bishop Fructuosus and his Deacons, Augurius and Eulogius* 2.

40. For more examples and a more complete discussion, see Kalantzis, *Caesar and the Lamb*, 60, 64–66, 120.

41. *Acts of Maximilian*; cf. Kalantzis, *Caesar and the Lamb*, 157–60.

42. *Acts of Marcellus*, 1; cf. Kalantzis, *Caesar and the Lamb*, 160–63.

43. *Martyrdom of St. Marinus*. Cf. Kalantzis, *Caesar and the Lamb*, 155–57. See also Tertullian's account (*De Corona* or *The Crown*) of a Roman soldier in Africa who refused to wear a crown honoring the emperor; cf. Kalantzis, *Caesar and the Lamb*, 120–22.

despicable act, better is it for me to become a sacrifice to the Lord Christ by my own choice rather than immolate myself to your idol Saturn."[44]

Suffering that Leads to Conversion

So far, we have established that the context of suffering afforded many early Christian the environment to share their faith verbally. Yet, is there evidence that such suffering led to non-Christians actually embracing the gospel? Tertullian of Carthage was convinced that suffering was directly connected to the growth of the church. In his *Apology,* he taunted the Roman authorities of Carthage: "But go zealously on . . . kill us, torture us, condemn us, grind us to dust; your injustice is the proof that we are innocent . . . the [more] often we are mown down by you, the more in number we grow; the blood of Christians is seed.[45]" Making an even greater claim, Tertullian continues: "For all who witness the noble patience of its martyrs, as struck with misgivings, are inflamed with desire to examine into the matter in question; and as soon as they come to know the truth, they straightway enroll themselves its disciples."[46]

While Tertullian's exaggerating tone renders some of his claims rather incredulous, there are, nevertheless, accounts of suffering in Christian literature that led to conversions to Christ during this period. Referring to his own spiritual journey in the *Second Apology,* Justin stated that he was compelled to faith in Christ in part because of the testimony of suffering Christians. He writes: "For I myself, too, when I was delighting in the doctrines of Plato, and heard the Christians slandered, and saw them fearless of death, and of all other-things which are counted fearful, perceived that it was impossible that they could be living in wickedness and pleasure."[47]

Throughout the account of Perpetua and Felicitas and companions, the group has regular contact with people in the prison, court, and amphitheater where a Christian testimony could be given. One character of interest is the chief prison officer Pudens who is mentioned multiple times in the *Passion of Perpetua and Felicitas.* Early in the narrative, we learn that he is impressed by the testimony of the Christians and shows them favor

44. *Martyrdom of Saintly Dasius,* 5; cf. Kalantzis, *Caesar and the Lamb,* 167–69.

45. Tertullian, *Apology,* 50.12–14 in ANF 3.

46. Tertullian, *To Scapula,* 5 in ANF 3; also Decret, *Early Christianity in North Africa,* 35.

47. Justin, *Second Apology,* 12 in ANF 1; cf. Justin, *First Apology,* 16.

by allowing them more visitors.[48] At a later point, the narrator reports that Pudens had actually come to faith: "the head of the prison was himself a Christian."[49] As Saturus was nearing death, he sought to strengthen Pudens the new believer by sharing: "Good-bye. Remember me, and remember the faith. These things should not disturb you but rather strengthen you."[50] While the group of believers apparently impacted workers like Pudens within the prison, they also seemed to have an effect on the curious crowds that came to see them at the prison. Describing what appear to be opportunities to preach, the narrator records that "they spoke to the mob with the same steadfastness, warned them of God's judgment, stressing the joy they would have in their suffering, and ridiculing the curiosity of those that came to see them." The account continues with an outcome that included conversions to faith: "Thus everyone would depart from the prison in amazement, and many of them began to believe."[51]

In the early third century in Egypt, a woman named Potamianea was arrested, tortured, and eventually executed for her Christian faith. Following her confession, the gathered mob began to hurl insults at her. In an interesting turn of events, Basilides, the Roman soldier tasked with leading her to the place of execution actually came to her defense. Her martyrdom account reads, "Basilides, showing her the utmost pity and kindness, prevented them and drove them off." The narrative continues as Potamianea "welcomed the sympathy shown her and urged the man to be of good heart: when she went to her Lord she would pray for him, and it would not be long before she would pay him back for all he had done for her." Sometime after Potamianea's martyrdom, Basilides refused to take a pagan oath with his fellow soldiers and it was discovered that he has become a Christian. As this became known, Basilides not only embraced Potamianea's Christian faith, but he also joined her as a martyr.[52]

Finally, let us consider the case of the first British martyr Alban, who was put to death during the Great Persecution. According to Bede: "though still a heathen at the time, [Alban] gave hospitality to a certain cleric who was fleeing from his persecutors. When Alban saw this man occupied day and night in continual vigils and prayers, divine grace suddenly shown

48. *Passion of Perpetua and Felicitas* 9.
49. Ibid., 16.
50. Ibid., 21.
51. Ibid., 17.
52. *Martyrdom of Potamiaena and Basilides.*

upon him and he learned to imitate his guest's faith and devotion."[53] Having embraced the gospel, Alban went a step farther and willfully took the place of the cleric when the police came to arrest him. The account continues with Alban being led across a river by his executioner when the river apparently dried up. Observing this miracle, the executioner threw down his sword—an apparent confession of faith in Christ—and joined Alban as a martyr.[54]

Many critics have alleged that such accounts of martyrdom have been touched up or are even fictitious and unreliable. Though admittedly some of the details are difficult to imagine, especially for modern readers, the simple point made by the authors of these accounts is that non-believers were coming to faith in Christ because of the effective witness of suffering Christians.

Singing Prisoners, a Baptized Guard

On August 3, 2001, Heather Mercer and Dayna Curry, Christian aid workers serving with the group Shelter Now, were arrested and imprisoned by the Taliban in Afghanistan. Following 105 days in captivity, Mercer and Curry's rescue (and that of their six co-workers) quickly became front page news in the United States. While speaking about her experience at Liberty University in 2009, Mercer shared that one of their keys to survival was worship. Each day, the group was allowed some time in the prison courtyard to get some fresh air—time that they used to sing worship songs and pray. Heather later learned that the Taliban soldier guarding them was apparently touched by their songs and overall resolve during captivity. After the Taliban's fall in Afghanistan, the guard traveled to Pakistan, sought out an evangelical pastor, and reportedly believed the gospel and was baptized. While Perpetua and other early Christian confessors apparently won some of their oppressors to Christ, it seems that Mercer and her colleagues had a similar impact on one Taliban guard.[55]

53. Bede, *Ecclesiastical History* 1.7.

54. Ibid., 1.7; also Thomas, *Christianity in Roman Britain,* 47–48.

55. Heather Mercer recounted this narrative on February 16, 2009, while speaking at the Liberty University Convocation. See "Missionary Heather Mercer Tells Story."

The Appealing Virtue of Suffering

Though it appears that martyrdom contributed directly to conversion in these instances, it seems that Christian confessors had a broader and more long-term impact because their suffering was a virtue that was ultimately appealing to their pagan and non-Christian audiences. Fox asserts that "in the early church, martyrdoms were exceptionally public events."[56] As we have shown, the audiences included not only the Roman authorities but also jeering and curious mobs. In the account of Montanus and Lucius, it was reported that "Montanus raised his arms to heaven and prayed in so loud a voice that not only all the faithful but even the pagans heard the sound."[57] In the martyrdoms of Marinus, Marcellus, Maximilian, and Julius, the pagan audience was comprised of members of the Roman army. Though focusing on the witness of suffering Christians in the first and second century, Irvin and Sunquist's observation seems to hold true for much of the pre-Constantine period. They write: "Especially effective in terms of evangelistic witness was the courage Christians often showed in the face of severe persecution or even death . . . Christian apologists continued to make the point that unlettered Christians demonstrated in their lives the virtues, especially courage, considered the sign of a true philosophy."[58] To support the claim that suffering was an appealing virtue that influenced many pagans toward gospel, let us consider several examples, including the martyrdom accounts of women and the elderly.

In the martyrdom narrative of the Spanish church leader Fructuosus, it was reported: "As Bishop Fructuosus was being taken to the amphitheater with his deacons, the people began to sympathize with him, for he was much beloved of pagans and Christians alike."[59] After Papylus and Carpus were burned alive by authorities in Pergamum, the predominantly pagan crowd apparently protested their treatment by exclaiming, "This is a harsh judgment and an unjust sentence."[60] Observing the torture experienced by Pionius and his companions, it was noted that some in the crowd sympathized, "what a terrible chastisement." Once returned to the prison, the

---

56. Fox, *Pagans and Christians*, 420.

57. *Martyrdom of Saints Montanus and Lucius* 15.

58. Irvin and Sunquist, *History of the World Christian Movement*, 37.

59. *Martyrdom of Bishop Fructuosus and His Deacons, Augurius and Eulogius* 3.

60. Cited in Frend, *Martyrdom and Persecution*, 201.

group apparently found favor with the prison guards and were moved out of the worst section of the jail to the best part.[61]

Eusebius' history of the martyrs of Palestine during the Diocletian persecution offers further support for the virtuous appeal of suffering Christians. Remembering the impact of a believer named Peter on the Roman officials, he writes: "Peter . . . appeared, a famous confessor of the kingdom of God; and so manfully did he behave in his struggle for the worship of God, and so victorious was he in the conflict of his martyrdom, that he even excited admiration in the judge himself."[62] Athanasius later affirmed that the suffering of Palestinian Christians during this period aroused the sympathies of the pagan observers.[63]

The impact on pagan audiences seemed especially powerful when the martyrs were women. From a cursory reading of the martyrdom literature, the persecution endured by women was quite extreme. In Egypt, Potamiaena suffered at the hands of the judge Aquila who "subjected her entire body to cruel torments, and then threatened to hand her over to his gladiators to assault her physically" and that "boiling pitch was slowly poured drop by drop over different parts of her body, from her toes to the top of her head."[64] Agape, Irene, and Chione were each burned at the stake in Thessalonica for refusing to eat food sacrificed to pagan idols.[65] In Tebessa in North Africa, the Prefect Anullinus seemed especially cruel in ordering Crispina to be tortured: "Let her be completely disfigured by having her hair cut and her head shaved with a razor till she is bald, that her beauty might first thus be brought to shame." Crispina courageously responded to this treatment: "I should be very happy to lose my head for the sake of my God. For I refuse to sacrifice to these ridiculous deaf and dumb statues."[66]

While such cruel actions alone surely encouraged sympathy from pagan audiences, other accounts argue for a more explicit connection. In a horrific account from Palestine, Eusebius describes an unnamed virgin from the town of Baishan:

> [She] had been brought by force from Baishan, and suffered insults and cruel tortures from the judge before she was condemned.

61. *Martyrdom of Pionius the Presbyter and His Companions* 10–11.
62. Eusebius, *History of the Martyrs in Palestine* 38.
63. Frend, *Martyrdom and Persecution*, 380.
64. *Martyrdom of Potamiaena and Basilides*.
65. *Martyrdom of Saints Agape, Irene, and Chinoe at Saloniki*.
66. *Martyrdom of Crispina* 3.

> This same blessed woman he stripped naked . . . in order that he might indulge his lustful eyes in looking at the rest of her limbs; and he carried her about through the whole city, being tortured with straps; and afterwards took her before the tribunal of the governor, where with great boldness of speech she made the confession of her faith—that she was a Christian; and there also displayed her courage and patience under every kind of torture; and was afterwards delivered over by the governor to be burnt with fire. Moreover, the same judge became day by day more ferocious . . . and of this same maiden of whom it has been just spoken, and of those who on the same day were consummated by confession, orders were issued that their bodies should be devoured by animals, and be carefully guarded night and day till they should be consumed by birds.[67]

Eusebius added that on account of the atrocities experienced by this woman and others that a "great sorrow and grief came even upon those who were aliens from us in the faith, because of these things which their own eyes beheld."[68]

Similarly, the famous account of Perpetua and Felicitas in Carthage is only magnified because they were young women. Perpetua came from an affluent and well-known family in Carthage and had given birth to a child just prior to her arrest. Felicitas was her servant and managed to give birth to a child in prison. According to the *Passion,* an assistant to the prison guard was particularly moved by Felicitas' circumstances as a new mother facing execution.[69] Perhaps the cruelty of the whole story is best captured when the women were taken into the Carthage amphitheater: "So they were stripped naked, placed in nets and thus brought out into the arena. Even the crowd was horrified when they saw that one was a delicate young girl and the other was a woman fresh from childbirth with the milk still dripping from her breasts. And so they were brought back again and dressed in unbelted tunics."[70] Ironically, the crowd demonstrated a level of sympathy for the women; however, they were not moved enough to demand an end the whole unjust affair.

67. Eusebius, *History of the Martyrs in Palestine* 35.

68. Ibid., 35

69. *Passion of Perpetua and Felicitas* 15.

70. Ibid., 20.

**Figure 4: Carthage ampitheatre where Felicitas and Perpetua
and others were put to death.**

One of the celebrated confessors among the martyrs of Lyons was a woman named Blandina. After being thrown in prison and initially tortured in the amphitheater, which she managed to survive, she was once again thrown to the beasts where she was beaten to death. Commenting on this series of events, Frend writes, "Those who watched her first tortures in the amphitheater are reported to have said 'that never among them had a woman suffered so much for so long.'"[71] Offering support to the central argument that suffering ultimately influenced pagans toward embracing the gospel, Frend adds, "Sometimes such thoughts proved to be the first stirrings towards acceptance of the Christian faith."[72]

Finally, the suffering of elderly Christians seems to have also had an impact on non-Christian observers. We can only imagine the response of those who saw the aging Conon bound and drug behind a horse on his way to execution.[73] Similarly, Eusebius recorded the public humiliation of Sylvanus of Gaza: "He, an old man, of a noble person, went down to the

71. Frend, *Martyrdom and Persecution*, 7–9.

72. Ibid., 9.

73. *Martyrdom of Saint Conon*, 2.

stadium, and there, in his first confession before the people of Caesarea, he acquitted himself valiantly, being tried with scourgings. And when he had endured these bravely, he fought in a second conflict, in which the old man endured the combs on his sides like a young man. And at the third conflict he was sent to the copper mines; and during a life of much length he exhibited great probation."[74]

While Conon and Sylvanus' testimonies surely had a moving effect on their audiences, the narrator of the *Martyrdom of Polycarp* makes a stronger case for the virtuous appeal of this elderly bishop. Apparently, the police were impressed with the eighty-six year old bishop's composure at the time of his arrest. His offer of hospitality and request for some time to pray surely strengthened his rapport with them.[75] Finally, during his trial, the governor also seems impressed with the graceful manner in which Polycarp conducted himself in suffering.[76]

The Malatya Martyrs

On April 18, 2007, Necati Ayden, Ughur Yuksel, and Tilman Geske welcomed a group of five young men into the office of their publishing house in Malatya, Turkey for a discussion about the gospel. Though the young men had requested the meeting on the pretense of wanting to know more about the Christian faith, their true motives quickly surfaced as they tied up the men, subjected them to gruesome torture, and then slit their throats. The death of Ayden and Yuksel, both Turkish pastors, along with their German colleague Geske sent a shock wave through the church in Turkey. In the aftermath of the tragedy as the murderers were arrested and an investigation ensued, there was a most unexpected development. The Turkish media came and interviewed Shemsa Ayden and Susanna Geske—wives of two of the slain men. "Shemsa said, 'We forgive them because Jesus forgave us.' 'And He said we should love our enemies,' Susanna said."[77] While the murders shocked the Christian community, these responses were carried by the major Turkish newspapers and media outlets and were transmitted to millions of Turks. Not unlike the appeal that early suffering Christians had on the pagan majority in society, the testimony of these widows certainly had an impression for the gospel among many of Turkey's seventy million people.

---

74. Eusebius, *History of the Martyrs in Palestine* 51.

75. *Martyrdom of Polycarp* 7.

76. Ibid., 12.

77. Thomas, "Malatya Martyrs."

Suffering Led to Apologetics

As we have shown, the context of persecution and martyrdom allowed some Christians the opportunity to bring a defense of the faith against Jewish, heretical, and pagan thought. In the late second century in Rome, a certain Lucius offered a different type of apologetic by challenging the rationality and lawfulness of the state arresting his fellow believer Ptolameus. He appealed to the court: "What is the charge? He has not been convicted of adultery, fornication, murder, clothes-stealing, robbery or any crime whatsoever; yet you have punished this man because he confesses the name of Christian."[78] Lucius' apologetic—essentially a defense of human conscience and freedom of religion—was echoed by several other Christian thinkers in the second and third century. In short, Christian suffering led to an apologetic literature that served as another form of Christian witness. Let us consider a few examples here.

Justin wrote his *First Apology* in the mid-second century around the time of Polcaryp's execution. Whether it made it into their hands or not, the treatise was addressed to the Emperor Antoninus Pius and his sons, whom Justin regarded as rational men.[79] Not unlike Lucius, he challenged the unlawful practice of persecuting Christians without examining their behavior. Indirectly, he was challenging the logic of the Emperor Trajan's policy of not hunting down Christians but then prosecuting them when they were brought before the authorities by the mob.[80] He argued against this policy by asserting that Christians were truly the best citizens of the Roman Empire. Answering the claims that Christians were atheists, cannibals, and sexually immoral, Justin took time to explain that Christians worshipped an invisible God, that the Lord's Supper was not a cannibal act but a memorial to Christ's broken body and shed blood, and that agape feasts were not an occasion for drunken immorality, but rather an environment of Christian fellowship. Justin added that Christianity was a rational faith and that paganism was actually the irrational belief system.[81] Interestingly, Justin closed the work by appealing rationally to his readers while also offering a prophetic warning: "If these things seem to you to be reasonable and true, honor them; but if they seem nonsensical despise them as nonsense, and

---

78. *Martyrdom of Ptolameus and Lucius.*

79. Justin, *First Apology* 2.

80. Ibid., 3, 5.

81. Ibid., 9.

do not decree death against those who have done no wrong, as you would against enemies. For we forewarn you, that you shall not escape the coming judgment of God, if you continue in your injustice and we ourselves will invite you to do that which is pleasing to God."[82]

Around 177, Justin's disciple Athenagoras addressed his *Plea for the Christians* to the Emperor Marcus Aurelius and his son Commodus. He opens with the complaint: "Although we do no wrong . . . you allow us to be harassed, plundered, and persecuted, the mob making war on us only because of our name."[83] Appealing to Marcus' interest in Stoic philosophy, Athenagoras asserted that the God of the Christian Scriptures was not completely unlike the Stoic notion of deity—that there is one God who is intricately related to the universe. He added that the best Hellenistic philosophers were also monotheists.

Similar to Justin, Athenagoras thoroughly answered the pagan charges of atheism by writing: "we are not atheists since we acknowledge one God, who is uncreated, eternal, invisible, impassible, incomprehensible, illimitable. He is grasped only by mind and intelligence, and surrounded by light, beauty, spirit, and indescribable power. By him the universe was created through his Word, was set in order and is held together."[84] He responded to the claim that Christians were sexually immoral by citing Jesus' words from the Sermon on the Mount to not look at a woman lustfully. Finally, he explained the mystery of Christ's incarnation and even offered some early Christian reflection on the doctrine of the Trinity. He writes: "We acknowledge a God, and a Son, His Logos, and a Holy Spirit, united in essence—the Father, Son, the Spirit, because the Son is the Intelligence, Reason, Wisdom of the Father, and the Spirit and effluence, as light from fire."[85]

Tertullian, the greatest Christian writer in the Latin-speaking church prior to Augustine, continued the practice of written apologetics to defend and clarify the gospel. In his *Apology*, written around 197, he also defended Christianity against baseless claims such as incest and cannibalism and explained how Christians conducted themselves during their worship assemblies. He further ridiculed the manner in which Christians were judged and tried for simply having the name *(nomen)* Christian.[86] In a later

82. Ibid., 68.

83. Athenagoras, *Plea for the Christians*, 1 (all translations cited in Ehrman, *After the New Testament*, 65–71).

84. Ibid., 10.

85. Ibid., 24.

86. "Apologeticum."

work, Tertullian wrote to the Proconsul Scapula warning him that God's judgment would come on those who persecute the church. Yet, he added that this warning should not be taken as a threat because it was based on the Christian virtue of loving one's enemies.[87] He writes: "We have sent, therefore, this tract to you in no alarm about ourselves, but in much concern for you and for all our enemies, to say nothing of our friends. For our religion commands us to love even our enemies, and to pray for those who persecute us, aiming at a perfection all its own, and seeking in its disciples something of a higher type than the commonplace goodness of the world. For all love those who love them; it is peculiar to Christians alone to love those that hate them."[88]

Suffering Strengthened the Church

In some cases, those that were persecuted seemed mindful that their suffering was occurring in the context of the global church and for the edification of it. Prior to Polycarp's arrest, he took time to pray for "the entire catholic church scattered throughout the world.[89] Also, it is interesting that the account of the martyrs of Lyons was addressed to believers in Asia and Phrygia, the home land of many of these Christians.[90] To be sure, this letter was written to inform the Asian Christians of their suffering but also to encourage them to stand firm in the faith. As we conclude our discussion on how suffering related to the mission of the early church, it seems that the accounts of persecution and martyrdom also served in part to inspire Christians to stand firm in their faith and to be witnesses in their own right in an often hostile world. Let us support this claim by exploring some of the key monuments to martyrdom—sacred biographies, saints' feast days, related sermons about martyrs, and also churches built at martyrs' tombs.

Heffernan notes that from the early church through the medieval period, some 8000 sacred biographies were written to commemorate the lives of saints.[91] Though dismissed by some scholars as mere hagiography and lacking historical value, the goal of these short biographies, many of which were accounts of martyrdom, was to teach faith through concrete

87. "Ad Scapulum."
88. Tertullian, *To Scapula* 1.
89. *Martyrdom of Polycarp* 8.
90. *Martyrs of Lyons* 1.
91. Heffernan, *Sacred Biography,* 12.

examples. That is, through hearing and reading these accounts, believers were encouraged to imitate (*imitatio*) the faith commitment of these saints and martyrs.[92] Addressing the community of believers in Smyrna, the author of the *Martyrdom of Polycarp* demonstrated this value by writing: "we love the martyrs as the disciples and imitators of the Lord, and rightly so because of their unsurpassed loyalty towards their king and master. May we too share with them as fellow disciples!" He concludes that Polycarp "was not only a great teacher but a conspicuous martyr, whose testimony, following the gospel of Christ, everyone desires to imitate."[93]

Similarly, the narrator of the *Passion of Perpetua and Felicitas* opens his account by asserting: "The deeds recounted about the faith in ancient times were proof of God's favor and achieved the spiritual strengthening of men as well; and they were set forth in writing precisely that honor might be rendered to God and comfort to men . . . should not then more recent examples be set down that contribute equally to both ends?"[94] The account of two other African martyrs, Montanus and Lucius, expresses the same purpose almost verbatim: "Duly these have been written down to be preserved for those to come, that just as we have taken examples and learned from the ancient writings, so too we may derive some profit from those of recent times."[95] Finally, the narrative of Marian and James was recorded "not because they wanted the glory of their martyr's crown to be arrogantly broadcast, but rather that the ordinary men who constituted God's people might be given strength in the test of their faith by the sufferings of those who had gone before."[96]

Many martyrs were continually remembered by the church as they were assigned feast days.[97] For example, Polycarp has been remembered by the church on February 23, Perpetua and Felicitas on March 7, and Cyprian on September 14. It was the practice of many church fathers to preach special sermons on these saints' days commemorating their testimonies and calling the church to imitate their faith. Among Augustine's 100 feast day sermons for martyrs, nine were dedicated to the memory of the martyred

---

92. Smither, "To Emulate and Imitate," 146–52.

93. *Martyrdom of Polycarp* 17, 19.

94. *Passion of Perpetua and Felicitas* 1.

95. *Martyrdom of Montanus and Lucius* 23.

96. *Martyrdom of Marian and James* 1.

97. See Wilken, *First Thousand Years*, 48.

bishop Cyprian.[98] In *Sermon* 311, Augustine admonished the church to maintain the focus of a saint's day: "the right way to celebrate the festivals of the martyrs should be by imitating their virtues. It's easy enough to celebrate in honor of a martyr; the great thing is to imitate the martyr's faith and patience."[99] In short, Augustine's purpose in preaching about Cyprian was not unlike that of the authors of sacred biographies—to encourage the imitation of faith.

A final way in which the faith of confessors was remembered by the church was through constructing church buildings on the site of their tombs. For instance, following Cyprian's martyrdom in Carthage in 258, a chapel was erected that was later expanded into a larger church facility. In his *Confessions,* Augustine mentions visiting this place with his mother prior to his conversion.[100] Perler adds that after Augustine was set apart as bishop of Hippo, he returned to Carthage and preached at least a few sermons in the church, including some of the noted feast day sermons commemorating Cyprian.[101] Commenting on a church building project in England that had a similar focus, Bede reported that "when peaceful Christian times returned, a church of wonderful workmanship was built, a worthy memorial of his [Alban's] martyrdom."[102] While on one hand, these church buildings at times facilitated an unhealthy cult of martyrs,[103] on the other, they served as a visible reminder of the winsome testimonies of faith that ought to be emulated.

In short, sacred biographies, sermons, and even church buildings told the stories of suffering Christians for the broader church. For many observing Christians, these accounts encouraged them to witness unto Christ through suffering. For others, these stories admonished them to stand firm for the gospel in turbulent environments, to invite non-Christians to faith in Christ, and ultimately to expand the church.

98. Augustine's feast day sermons are found in volumes 9–10 of Rotelle, *Works of Saint Augustine* (WSA). His sermons on Cyprian are *Sermons* 309–313, 313A–E. See my synopsis of each of these sermons in Smither, "'To Emulate and Imitate,'" 153–55.

99. Augustine, *Sermon* 311.1. Unless otherwise noted, all English translations of Augustine's sermons are from WSA.

100. Augustine, *Confessions* 5.8.15.

101. Perler, *Les Voyages de Saint Augustin,* 440–76.

102. Bede, *Ecclesiastical History* 1.7.

103. Thomas, *Christianity in Roman Britain,* 156.

Conclusion

Preaching on suffering and God's redemptive plan, Gregory the Great stated: "The Father sent his Son, appointing him to become a human person for the redemption of the human race. He willed him to come into the world to suffer—and yet he loved his Son whom he sent to suffer. The Lord is sending his chosen apostles into the world, not to the world's joys but to suffer as he himself was sent. Therefore as the Son is loved by the Father and yet is sent to suffer, so also the disciples are loved by the Lord, who nevertheless sends them into the world to suffer."[104]

In many respects, Gregory has summarized some of the main arguments in this chapter. First, the Christian movement was birthed through suffering in the work of Christ. Second, suffering in the form of persecution and martyrdom seemed to accelerate the spread of the gospel. This occurred as Christians, in the midst of their suffering, verbally confessed their allegiance to Christ, clarified the gospel, and defended the faith against non-Christian and heretical thought. In some cases, these defenses turned into written treatises that had a broader impact for the gospel. According to some accounts, the testimonies of persecuted Christians were instrumental in the immediate conversion of non-believers, while in other instances, it seems that the virtue of suffering did have an appeal that prepared the way for many pagans to embrace the gospel. Finally, as the accounts of Christian martyrs were remembered by the church through sacred biographies, sermons, and even church buildings, these faith stories encouraged believers to stand firm in their faith and to continue to witness unto Christ.

Questions for Reflection

1. Read Matthew 10:16–23:

    "Behold, I am sending you out as sheep in the midst of wolves, so be wise as serpents and innocent as doves. Beware of men, for they will deliver you over to courts and flog you in their synagogues, and you will be dragged before governors and kings for my sake, to bear witness before them and the Gentiles. When they deliver you over, do not be anxious how you are to speak or what you are to say, for what you are to say will be given to you in that hour. For it is not you who speak, but the Spirit of your Father speaking through you. Brother will deliver brother over to death, and the father his child, and children will rise against parents and have them put

---

104. Gregory the Great, *Forty Gospel Homilies* 26, cited in Crosby and Oden, *Ancient Christian Devotional*, Kindle Locations 967–70.

to death, and you will be hated by all for my name's sake. But the one who endures to the end will be saved. When they persecute you in one town, flee to the next, for truly, I say to you, you will not have gone through all the towns of Israel before the Son of Man comes."

How did the early suffering Christians identify with Jesus' words in this passage?

2. What can modern Christians learn from the verbal witness (confession of faith, gospel clarification, apologetics) of persecuted Christians in the early church?

3. What hope or encouragement might today's persecuted Christians glean from the testimonies of these early Christians?

4. Some early Christian apologists such as Justin and Tertullian denounced the unlawful arrest and persecution of Christians. What would that look like today?

5. The early church remembered martyred Christians through sacred biographies, feast days, sermons, and even buildings. In what ways can the modern church remember and preserve the faith stories of suffering believers past and present?

4

Evangelism

IN 1930, A GROUP OF Protestant laymen led by Harvard professor William Hocking met in New York to evaluate the previous century of global missions. While many of the study's findings—published as *Re-thinking Missions* in 1932—were quite insightful, one noticeable element was its conclusions about evangelism in the work of mission. Essentially redefining evangelism, they wrote, "Ministry to the secular needs of men . . . is evangelism, in the right sense of the word." Reflecting the tendency of late nineteenth-century liberal theology, which diminished the spiritual and eternal qualities of Christian conversion, the group commented further on the future of mission practice: "We believe that the time has come to set the educational and other philanthropic aspects of mission work free from organized responsibility to the work of conscious and direct evangelism."[1] In short, as evangelism was being redefined as humanization, historic gospel proclamation (*kerygma*) was being eliminated from the theology and practice of mission.

On the contrary, when the delegates of the Lausanne Congress on World Evangelization met in Switzerland nearly a half century later in 1974, they articulated a statement on evangelism that was decidedly different from that of the Hocking report:

> To evangelize is to spread the good news that Jesus Christ died for
> our sins and was raised from the dead according to the Scriptures,

---

1. Hocking, *Re-thinking Missions*, 326.

and that as the reigning Lord he now offers the forgiveness of sins and the liberating gifts of the Spirit to all who repent and believe ... evangelism itself is the proclamation of the historical, biblical Christ as Savior and Lord, with a view to persuading people to come to him personally and so be reconciled to God ... the results of evangelism include obedience to Christ, incorporation into his Church and responsible service in the world.[2]

This article from the Lausanne Covenant certainly captured more of the essence of historic Christianity and, of course, the values of evangelicalism that include the authority of Scripture, the central role of the cross, and the necessity of conversion. Further, if mission no longer includes proclamation, then it can no longer be called mission. To be sure, if the church fathers were reading the Hocking report and the Lausanne Covenant, they would certainly resonate more with the latter with respect to evangelism.

What is evangelism? Not unlike the Lausanne writers, Bosch defines it as "the proclamation of salvation in Christ to those who do not believe in him, calling them to repentance and conversion, announcing forgiveness of sin, and inviting them to become living members of Christ's earthly community and to begin a life of service to others in the power of the Holy Spirit."[3] The foundational elements of the gospel (*euangelion*) or what was proclaimed (*kerygma*) are probably best articulated by Paul in 1 Corinthians 15:3–5: "that Christ died for our sins in accordance with the Scriptures, that he was buried, that he was raised on the third day in accordance with the Scriptures, and that he appeared to Cephas, then to the twelve."[4] In fact, Flemming argues that the four New Testament Gospels are best understood as commentaries on the life of Jesus that are heavily oriented toward the last week of his life.[5] In an insightful recent work, Scott McKnight continually asserts that the "'Gospel'" is the Story of Jesus that fulfills, completes, and resolves Israel's Story" and in turn flows to all peoples and nations.[6] While much scholarly discussion has been given to the essence of the apostolic message (*kerygma*), Green helpfully concludes that "the gospel is good

2. "Lausanne Covenant," 4.

3. Bosch, *Transforming Mission*, 10–11.

4. 1 Cor 15:3–5.

5. Flemming, *Contextualization in the New Testament*, 234.

6. McKnight, *King Jesus Gospel*, 51.

news; it is proclamation; it is witness" regarding the person and work of Christ.[7]

In this chapter, we will explore how the early church approached evangelism. In chapter 2, we established that there were active full-time, bivocational, and rather anonymous missionaries, meaning that mission and evangelism were in the DNA of the early church. In addition to itinerant preaching, already discussed in chapter 2, we will begin by considering some other prominent forms of evangelism. Though it will be discussed in more detail in chapter 8, it should be noted here that much of evangelism in the early church happened in the context of the existing church and included proclamation, catechesis, and baptism. In the present chapter, however, we will focus more on community evangelism and then the strategy of sharing testimonies and telling faith stories. After, we will consider some specific contexts and audiences for evangelism including intellectuals, political leaders, and even heretics.

Community Evangelism

Evangelism can be observed in the early church through the witness of Christians who were integrated into the fabric of society. As shown, the pre-Constantinian Christian movement in the Roman Empire experienced sporadic and varying degrees of discrimination and persecution from the greater pagan society and, at times, even from the imperial authorities. Though Christian communities largely met in homes prior to the fourth century and others possibly gathered under the creative guise of a funerary association, one should not assume that Christians were segregated or marginalized from the greater society. Pliny's observation about Christians in second-century Bithynia and Tertullian's claims about second- and third-century Carthage indicate otherwise. Valerian and Diocletian's pogroms against the church, which included purges of the Senate, confiscating property from the wealthy, and even arresting royal family members, also show that Christians were quite integrated into daily Roman life.[8] As mentioned,

---

7. Green, *Evangelism in the Early Church,* 77. For an expanded discussion of the essence of the proclaimed gospel, see 76–115; McKnight, *King Jesus Gospel,* 45–54; and Patzia, *Making of the New Testament,* 55–56.

8. Fox, *Pagans and Christians,* 43, 66; Sordi, *Christians and the Roman Empire,* 83, 114, 125; Frend, *Martyrdom and Persecution,* 106, 110; and Kreider, "'They Alone Known the Right Way to Live,'" 171.

the claims of the second-century *Epistle to Diognetus*—that Christians "inhabit both Greek and barbarian cities . . . participate in all things as citizens . . . live on earth but participate in the life of heaven"[9]—reveal an apparent spirit of early Christian evangelism. That is, Christians testified to their eternal hope from their position as fully committed citizens in the earthly city.

Recorded Testimonies

As Christians engaged the pagan society around them, a further form of witness was through sharing testimonies and telling the faith stories of others. One of the earliest recorded Christian testimonies was Luke's narration of Paul telling his conversion story to a hostile mob in Jerusalem. In his speech, Paul attempts to identify with his Jewish audience by speaking to them in Hebrew, by highlighting his own Jewish background, and by admitting his own initial hostility toward Christians. Afterward, he recounts his dramatic conversion story—largely a retelling of the events of Acts 9— and then continues with a straightforward account of his post-conversion life prior to being shouted down by the crowd.[10]

In the first eight chapters of the transcript of his *Dialogue with Trypho*, Justin recounts his journey to faith. The philosopher-evangelist also endeavored to connect with his audience—philosophically minded readers or listeners—by narrating his experiences in various schools of Greek philosophy. His conversion story comes to a climax when he meets an aged man by the seashore who challenges Justin's belief about Plato and introduces him to the Hebrew prophets and the Messiah. Only after believing in Christ does Justin realize that he has become a true philosopher.[11]

In the eighth book of his *Confessions*, Augustine shares one of the most stirring conversion accounts in the early church period. The final stage of his conversion experience includes several intriguing features. First, he vividly relates the psychological and emotional battle that went on within him in the garden near Milan. He writes: "When I was making up my mind to serve the Lord my God . . . I was the one who wanted to follow that course, and I was the one who wanted not to."[12] Second, up until the very

9. *Epistle to Diognetus* 5.1–6, cited in Schnabel, *Early Christian Mission*, 2:1566.

10. Acts 21:37—22:22.

11. Justin, *Dialogue with Trypho* 2–8; also Justin, *Second Apology* 12.

12. Augustine, *Confessions* 8.10.22 (all translations are from WSA).

end of the garden experience, Augustine was in the company of his friend Alypius; so, the spiritual struggle was not an individual one. In fact, immediately after confessing Christ, Augustine went inside and told his mother about his experience. Finally, from the famous "pick it up and read" (*tolle lege*) narrative, we learn that Scripture—in this case Paul's letters—played a central role leading up to and encompassing the moment of Augustine's conversion experience.[13]

In recounting his conversion story in *Confessions,* Augustine goes further and narrates the faith stories of four other converts. These were testimonies that clearly encouraged him on his journey to faith that Augustine in turn uses to influence his readers toward the gospel. He begins by declaring that he will "not pass over in silence" how Simplicianus (d. 400) told him the conversion story of the philosopher and rhetor, Marius Victorinus (b. 300). Victorinus, who had been a pagan, became convinced of the truth of the gospel through reading the Scriptures. Simplicianus, who personally witnessed to Victorinus, urged him to forsake his public reputation and declare his faith in the context of the church. As a result, he enrolled as a catechumen, was baptized, and publicly confessed his faith before the church assembly.[14]

Augustine interpreted Simplicianus' intentions for telling the story by writing: "I was fired to imitate Victorinus; indeed it was to this end that your servant Simplicianus had related it."[15] Indeed, Augustine had much in common with Victorinus, as both men were interested in philosophy, were on a similar career path, had concerns about their public reputation, and had an interest in the Christian Scriptures. Hence, Augustine was encouraged to pursue Christian faith because Victorinus had.[16]

In the middle of Simplicianus' narrative, including Augustine's take on Simplicianus' motives, Augustine pauses and offers a prayerful commentary that seems very much intended for his own readers: "Come, Lord, arouse us and call us back, kindle us and seize us, prove to us how sweet you are in your burning tenderness; let us love you and run to you. Are there not many who return to you from a deeper, blinder pit than did Victorinus,

13. Ibid., 8.8.19; 8.11.27; 8.12.29–30.

14. Ibid., 8.2.3–5.

15. Ibid., 8.5.10.

16. For a helpful discussion on parallels between the conversion experiences of Victorinus and Augustine, especially regarding the relationship between humility and baptism in both men's spiritual journeys, see Alexander, *Augustine's Early Theology of the Church,* 67–79.

many who draw near to you and are illumined as they become children of God?"[17] Could it be that Augustine was also reaching out to his philosophically minded, career-oriented readers who could relate to both Victorinus and Augustine?

In the very next passage, Augustine tells of a visit from Ponticianus, a Roman functionary, who told Augustine and Alypius about the Egyptian monk Antony. While recounting Antony's call to the ascetic life, Ponticianus also related the story of two Roman officials from Trier, who after reading Athanasius' *Life of Antony*, resigned from their posts in order to pursue an ascetic lifestyle. Augustine, intrigued by the accounts, wrote: "even while he [Ponticianus] spoke, you [God] were wrenching me back toward myself . . . that I might perceive my sin and hate it."[18]

Ponticianus' account connected with Augustine for a number of reasons. First, there was possibly a cultural connection because Ponticianus was an African who was telling the faith story of another African (Antony) to two other Africans (Augustine and Alypius) in Milan. Second, Antony's conversion to an ascetic lifestyle—as well as the similar conversion of the officials from Trier—was meaningful for Augustine because one of his biggest obstacles to faith was sexual immorality. In fact, Augustine introduced the entire Ponticianus encounter with this prayerful commentary: "Now I will relate how you set me free from a craving for sexual gratification."[19] Third, Augustine, who had been quite infatuated with career ambitions, identified with the two officials who set aside their careers for the sake of the gospel. At the conclusion of his conversion account, Augustine testified that he was "no longer . . . entertaining any worldly hope."[20] As a result, he also resigned from his imperial post before moving back to Africa to pursue a monastic lifestyle.[21]

While his account of Simplicianus' story of Marius Victorinus impacted some readers, Augustine's narrative of Ponticianus telling the story of Antony and the two officials probably reached others with the gospel. Surely, there were those whose career ambitions were poisoning their spiritual lives, while others struggled like Augustine with sexual immorality. Perhaps Augustine's African readers were especially attracted to the African

17. Augustine, *Confessions* 8.4.9.
18. Ibid., 8.7.17.
19. Ibid., 8.6.13.
20. Ibid., 8.12.30.
21. Ibid., 9.2.2.

angle of Ponticianus' story. Hence, the example of Antony, the two officials, and now Augustine provided models for imitation.

Augustine's testimony in *Confessions* is one of the most celebrated conversion accounts from the early church. Moreover, by narrating faith stories within his own faith story, Augustine does seem to have an evangelistic purpose for his late fourth- and early fifth-century readers, who could probably identify with at least one of the characters mentioned in Augustine's narrative.

Evangelizing Intellectuals

As Christians in our period of study were surely communicating the gospel on all levels of society—to the educated and non-educated alike—some early Christian evangelists were particularly focused on reaching intellectuals. As shown, Justin and his disciples Athenagoras and Aristides—moved by the circumstances of discrimination and persecution against Christians— addressed their apologetics in a very rational manner. Toward the end of his *First Apology,* Justin affirmed to his pagan audience in a polite yet clear manner, "we do not hate you but we wish to convert you."[22]

Mission to Intellectuals

This was the title of the January 11, 1960 Time magazine article devoted to the ministry of Francis Schaeffer (1912–1984).[23] Along with his wife Edith, Schaeffer was a Presbyterian missionary to Switzerland beginning in the late 1940s. Coming from the United States where his biggest concerns were safeguarding the authority of Scripture and historic Christian doctrine, in Switzerland, Schaeffer encountered many young people and students who doubted the existence of God or who struggled to make sense of the meaning of life. While hosting such guests at L'Abri, their home in the Swiss Alps, the Schaeffers showed hospitality, patiently listened to the difficult questions, and sought to offer a reasonable answer rooted in biblical Christianity. This would ultimately lead Schaeffer toward a speaking and writing ministry that would have a global impact and ultimately provide a model for evangelical Christians to engage the world around them with the gospel.

---

22. Justin, *First Apology* 57.2.

23. "Mission to Intellectuals," 62–63.

Similarly, Theophilus of Antioch (d. ca. 190), another disciple of Justin's, engaged his pagan friend Autolycus in thoughtful and respectful dialogue. Through the course of three written works, Theophilus shares his testimony of embracing the gospel through reading the Scriptures, communicates God's attributes, and also shows the need for man to repent and experience moral transformation.[24] In short, Theophilus' goal in writing was "to provide an attractive invitation to a Christian way of life."[25]

In Alexandria, we have shown that Pantaenus, who was trained in Stoic philosophy, ministered and led the catechetical school in a Gnostic context. According to Eusebius, his mission to India was also directed toward reaching philosophers.[26] After Pantaenus' departure around 200, Clement continued to lead the school and to teach the gospel in a city that was quite influenced by Greek philosophy and Gnosticism.[27]

Origen's work *Against Celsus* is yet another example of mission toward intellectuals. Around 178, Celsus, an Egyptian Platonic philosopher had written *On True Doctrine* in which he attacked Christians for preying on the simple and uneducated. Though demonstrating a level of familiarity with the New Testament Scriptures, Celsus claimed that Jesus was a magician and that the church, which he acknowledged was enjoying growth, was a secret and illegal society. The biggest problem that Celsus had with Christianity was its exclusive nature—that the ways of the divine had been revealed through a particular people. Though Origen wrote *Against Celsus* some seventy years later, the work was still relevant because many philosophically minded opponents of Christianity continued to share Celsus' sentiments.[28] Origen replied to these critics as a Christian Platonist—one who had plundered the Egyptians and used their philosophical framework to show that Christianity was indeed rational.[29] Though acknowledging the superiority of the Scriptures (divine philosophy) to Greek philosophy, he argued that the general knowledge of the divine played an important role in leading one to a divine philosophy. In short, Origen ably answered philosophical objections to the gospel by using philosophy and in turn gave Christianity some credibility among intellectuals. Suggesting that Origen

24. Rogers, "Theophilus of Antioch," 55–61.

25. Ibid., 63.

26. Eusebius, *Church History* 5.1–4.

27. Irvin and Sunquist, *History of the World Christian Movement*, 89.

28. Frend, *Martyrdom and Persecution*, 205–12.

29. Wilken, *First Thousand Years*, 63.

was the first Christian thinker and apologist to effectively engage with the broader culture around him, Wilken summarizes, "When [Origen] began to write, even philosophers knew he was someone to be reckoned with."[30]

Engaging Political Leaders

One of the tendencies observed in much of the early church period was that missionaries engaged political leaders in the process of evangelism.[31] While Christian writers such as Justin and Tertullian communicated elements of the gospel in their polemical works toward leaders, and many suffering Christians witnessed unto Christ before the authorities in the context of martyrdom, this trend is most apparent in the period following Constantine's rise to power. Generally, when a new field of mission was entered, many missionaries called upon the leader, communicated the gospel, and also sought favor to preach the gospel.[32]

The earliest and perhaps clearest example occurred in Armenia in the late third and early fourth century. According to Agathangelos, the Armenian chronicler who wrote *History of the Armenians,* Gregory the Enlightener had come to the region but was imprisoned for more than a decade by King Tiridates. Apparently Tiridates, his household, and many residents of his city were attacked by demons and began to go mad. Gregory was summoned from prison, prayed for the king, and proclaimed the gospel to him. As a result, Tiridates converted to Christianity, was baptized, and then commanded the people of Armenia to be baptized as well. Though the Armenian story preceded Constantine's conversion and the subsequent fourth-century Christianizing of the Roman Empire, Agathangelos recorded that Tiridates was delighted to hear of the Roman emperor's conversion and even visited him. Hence, the Armenian historian makes a deliberate link between the faiths of these two Christian monarchs.[33]

This pattern was further apparent in the fifth and sixth centuries in missions efforts in the British Isles. Commenting on the fifth century approach of Patrick of Ireland, George Hunter helpfully remarks, "Upon arrival at a tribal settlement, Patrick would engage the king and other opinion

30. Ibid., 55.

31. Jenkins, *Lost History of Christianity,* 68; Wilken, *First Thousand Years,* 357.

32. Ibid., 2–3.

33. See Agathangelos, *History of the Armenians,* in Coakley and Sterk, eds., *Readings in World Christian History,* 122–30.

leaders, hoping for their conversion, or at least their clearance, to camp near the people and form into a community of faith adjacent to the tribal settlement."[34] Gouddard adds, "We find Patrick everywhere setting himself first of all to convert the great."[35] In addition to the favor to proclaim the gospel, Patrick also hoped to receive land on which to build a church.

Columba, who came from a noble background and was probably accustomed to interacting with tribal leaders, continued this trend in sixth-century Scotland. As shown in chapter 2, Columba found favor with the Pictish King Brute, who converted to Christianity, allowed Columba the freedom to preach among the Picts, and also gave the monks land on which to build a monastery.[36] Though the Iona community seemed isolated, Columba continued to influence political issues in Scotland and Ireland and his biographer Adomnan notes that he openly prayed for a certain Aiden to become king.[37] Despite enjoying favor among the Picts in the sixth century, the Columban monks were expelled for a time in 710 following conflict with the Pictish leaders.[38]

Around 635, King Oswald of Northumbria returned from exile to claim his throne. Having spent the period of exile at Iona where he converted to Christianity, the new king was quite interested in having Christian missionaries teach his subjects in Northumbria. As a result, Aiden, one of Columba's disciples, was summoned for this task. In addition to having the freedom to preach, the monk was given land where he established the famous monastery at Lindisfarne.[39] In this case, the missional initiative came from a monarch following his conversion.

34. Hunter, *Celtic Way of Evangelism*, 21.

35. Gouddard, *Christianity in Celtic Lands*, 38–39; also Wilken, *First Thousand Years*, 271.

36. Blocher and Blandenier, *Evangelization of the World*, 68.

37. Adomnan, *Life of St. Columba* 1.8; 3.5.

38. Sharpe, Introduction, *Life of St. Columba*, 76.

39. Bede, *Ecclesiastical History* 3.3; Adomnan, *Life of St. Columba* 1.1; and Ward and Evans, "The Medieval West," 113.

Figure 5: Chapel where Columba is believed to be buried at Iona.

Similarly, as shown, Augustine of Canterbury made favorable contact with King Ethelbert of Kent at the end of the sixth century, which resulted in the king being converted along with a large number of his subjects. As a result, the monks were allowed to establish a monastery and build church facilities. While the ministry of Augustine was not insignificant,

King Ethelbert was probably already open to the gospel and favorable to the monks because his wife Bertha was already a Christian.[40]

A final example of missionaries engaging political leaders in the process of evangelism comes from sixth-century Africa. In part of his *Ecclesiastical History*, John of Ephesus narrates the conversion of the Numidian kingdoms (modern Egypt and Sudan). Interestingly, the account shows the disagreement between the Emperor Justinian and his wife Theodora over the Chalcedonian formula regarding the natures of Christ, which resulted in their rival efforts to send missionaries to Numidia. What is significant for our purposes is that the presbyter Julian, the original visionary for the mission and the key evangelist, began his work by making contact with the king of Noboadæ. John adds that Julian spent two years among them and that "he endured it patiently, and taught them, and baptized both the king and his nobles, and many of the people also."[41] He adds, "And when the people of Alodæi heard of the conversion of the Noboadæ, their king sent to the king of Noboadæ, requesting him to permit the bishop who had taught and baptized them, to come and instruct them in like manner."[42] Hence, while one Numidian king welcomed Julian's Christian mission, a second king invited him to come and teach his people the gospel.

Evangelizing Heretics

A final group evangelized by the early church were heretics—those who fell outside of the realm of historic Christian orthodoxy. In some respects similar to those reaching intellectuals, the evangelists who focused on heretics were engaging in mission across ideological and worldview frontiers. Also, as many heretics were present within the church, mission efforts toward them constituted part of the continual effort to evangelize the church. Let us consider a few representative examples.

As shown, Irenaeus of Lyons ministered in a third-century context that was greatly plagued by Gnostic thinking. Through key writings such as *Against All Heresies* and *Demonstration of the Apostolic Teaching*, he defended the gospel both in Gaul and at Rome.[43] Attacking Gnostic thinking for its most general claim, "the denial that the Creator is the God and Father

40. Irvin and Sunquist, *History of the World Christian Movement*, 327–28.
41. Cited in Coakley and Sterk, eds., *Readings in World Christian History*, 189.
42. Ibid., 190.
43. Eusebius, *Church History* 5.20.1–8.

of all,"[44] Irenaeus' approach, particularly through *Against All Heresies* was fourfold. First, he spent the first three chapters of the work carefully laying out the tenets of Gnostic thinking, a skill he had developed from spending nearly twenty years studying in Gnostic schools. Second, he argued for the baseless and mythological foundations of Gnosticism. Third, he challenged the Gnostic claims that they had a historical relationship to Jesus. Certainly, Irenaeus' personal connection to John the Evangelist (the Lord's disciple) through Polycarp strengthened his case. Finally, he ridiculed the unreasonable Gnostic approach to interpreting Scripture.[45] In sum, in his proclamation against the Gnostics, he appealed to the authority of Scripture, apostolic authority, and an inherited Trinitarian doctrine of God.[46]

Sharing Jesus, Not Christianity

Over the past two centuries, and increasingly over the past generation, there has been a concerted effort on the part of many evangelical Christians to proclaim the gospel among Muslims. Given the pioneering nature of missions to the Muslim world—a generally resistant area where the response has been slow—practitioners have arrived at many different opinions on how to evangelize Muslims. One interesting approach has been taken by Carl Medearis, who lived among Arab-Muslims in Lebanon for twelve years. Medearis believes that one should avoid talking about Christianity as a religion and simply focus on Jesus. In his most recent book, *Speaking of Jesus: The Art of Not-Evangelism*, Medearis relates, "While others are explaining and defending various isms and ologies we're simply pointing people to our friend. The one who uncovers and disarms. Who leads people right to himself. The beginning and the end of the story. A good story indeed."[47] How does Medearis' approach compare to that of John of Damascus?

A second example of evangelizing the church was Augustine's engagement with the Donatists—an African schismatic movement that began in the early fourth century in protest of the alleged moral laxness of catholic church leadership.[48] While most observers today would not conclude that the group was necessarily heretical, Augustine regarded them as such. In

---

44. Minns, "Irenaeus," 39.

45. Irenaeus, *Against All Heresies* 1.8, 23–27.

46. Hastings, *World History of Christianity*, 29.

47. Medearis, *Speaking of Jesus*, 38.

48. The most thorough treatment of Donatism continues to be W. H. C. Frend's mid-twentieth century book *The Donatist Church*.

his work *On Heresies*, Augustine described a point in which the Donatists' "stubborn dissent had grown strong [and] they turned their schism into heresy."[49] How did they cross this line? First, he objected to their practice of re-baptizing catholics—a violation of his doctrines of salvation, baptism, and church. Second, their schism became heresy because they were bringing division to the Lord's church. Finally, Augustine considered them heretics because they were led by a heretic. In this case, he alleged that Donatus, one of the movement's original leaders, held to a less than orthodox view of the Trinity.[50]

Because the Donatists were ordered by the Roman authorities to unite with the catholic church in 405 and again in 411 following the council of Carthage, some may argue that Augustine's actions toward the schismatic group should not be regarded as missional. Despite Augustine's approval of the government's actions, largely due to the violent elements within the movement, his engagement with the Donatists was largely persuasive in nature. Between 392 and 411, Augustine wrote seventeen letters and seven books to the Donatists while also making multiple visits to dialogue with their leaders about the origins of the schism and the true nature of the church. Further, in three church councils at Carthage between 401 and 403, Augustine encouraged catholic church leaders to engage their Donatist counterparts in dialogue. Augustine's words in *Letter* 34 (ca. 396–97) seem to capture the spirit of his engagement: "God knows that this attitude of my mind is directed toward peace and that I am not trying to force anyone involuntarily into the catholic communion, but to reveal the plan of truth to all who are in error. Then, once our ministry has made it evident with God's help, the very truth may be enough to persuade them to embrace and follow her."[51]

Though Augustine approved of the government's legislation against the Donatists in 411, he continued to approach them in a persuasive manner following this decision. From 411 to 419, Augustine wrote two more letters and three books to the Donatists in order to clarify the doctrinal issues. What is even more significant is that in 418, at the age of sixty-four, Augustine traveled 1100 kilometers across North Africa to meet with the Donatist Bishop Emeritus of Mauretania Caesarea who had refused to unite with the church. Aside from preaching to Emeritus' congregation, the two

---

49. Augustine, *On Heresies* 69.1 (all translations of Augustine's works are from WSA).

50. Augustine, *Against the Letter of Parmenian*; also Evans, "Heresy, Schism," 425.

51. Augustine, *Letter* 34.

engaged in a public dialogue and, in the end, Emeritus still refused to unite with the church. Hence, without any help or force from the government, Augustine appealed to Emeritus—without success—through reason.

In summary, Augustine engaged the Donatists in a fairly consistent manner for nearly three decades. Through letters, books, and visits, his interaction with the Donatists was marked by patient teaching that often involved repeating the same conversations. Though branding them as a heretical sect, Augustine still seemed to regard them as distant brothers. Hence, his mission to them was an example of evangelizing the church.[52]

Let us consider one more example. In chapter 1, we noted that a significant challenge to the growth and health of seventh- and eighth-century global Christianity, particularly in the East, was the rise of Islam.[53] Though Islam is viewed today as its own religion and one of the three chief monotheistic faiths, at least one church father considered the new movement to be a Christian heresy. Yanah ibn Mansur ibn Sarjun (ca. 650–749), better known as John of Damascus, was an Arab Christian who grew up under the Umayyad Dynasty, which was based at Damascus.[54] Like his father, John worked in the court of the caliph, probably serving as a type of accountant. Around 726, after thirty years of service in Damascus, he retired to the Mar Saba monastery near Jerusalem.

It was during this period that John wrote his most famous work, *Fount of Knowledge*. In part two of the book, he discussed a group of heresies— one of which was Islam or what he called "the Heresy of the Ishmaelites." In particular, John criticized Muhammad for teaching that God has no son while also castigating the movement for its practice of polygamy. In defense of historic, Nicene Christianity, John argued that Jesus was the inseparable Word and Spirit of God and that the Godhead should be understood as the mutual indwelling of the Father, Son, and Holy Spirit.[55]

When compared with the ministry of the Timothy of Baghdad, an Arab Christian leader who enjoyed a two-day dialogue with Muslim leaders in 781, John's approach was much more polemical and far less personal.[56] It

52. For a more expanded discussion of Augustine and the Donatists, see my forthcoming chapter, "Augustine, A Missionary to Heretics?"

53. Irvin and Sunquist, *History of the World Christian Movement*, 276.

54. One of the most helpful recent works on John and his engagement of Muslims is Daniel Janosik's, "John of Damascus: First Apologist to the Muslims."

55. Irvin and Sunquist, *History of the World Christian Movement*, 280–84.

56. Ibid., 284–87; Jenkins, *Lost History of Christianity*, 16–18.

should also be noted that John articulated his anti-Muslim polemic in writing from the rather secure location of the Mar Saba monastery. That said, John's engagement with Muslims in the eighth century was significant for a few reasons. First, his book not only offers a Christian perspective on the movement—that it was heretical and not necessarily a rival religion—but it also serves as an early historical commentary on Islam. Indeed, John's *Fount of Knowledge* precedes the Muslim Ibn Ishaq's biography of Muhammad (*Sirat Rasul Allah*) by at least thirty years, though the latter did not begin to circulate widely until the early ninth century.[57] Second, John's theological and apologetic method did pave the way for other evangelists to Muslims such as Timothy and Theodore Abu Qurrah (ca. 750–ca. 823).[58] Finally, John's polemical approach probably set the tone for Christian missions to Muslims until well into the nineteenth century.

Conclusion

In this chapter, we have argued that early Christian mission was characterized by a great commitment to kerygmatic proclamation. Indeed, evangelism was a central priority to mission during this period. To support this claim, we have discussed a few examples of evangelism strategies while also focusing on some of the audiences that were hearing the gospel. While sharing testimonies and even engaging intellectuals with the gospel are probably familiar to modern Christians, a commitment to church-based evangelism and approaching political leaders before preaching the gospel might give us pause for reflection.

Questions for Reflection

1. Read Acts 22:3–16

   And [Paul] said: "I am a Jew, born in Tarsus in Cilicia, but brought up in this city, educated at the feet of Gamaliel according to the strict manner of the law of our fathers, being zealous for God as all of you are this day. I persecuted this Way to the death, binding and delivering to prison both men and women, as the high priest and the whole council of elders can bear me witness. From them I received letters to the brothers, and I journeyed toward Damascus to take those also who were there and bring them in bonds to Jerusalem to be punished. As I was on my way

---

57. Janosik, "John of Damascus," 37, 43.
58. Ibid., 2.

and drew near to Damascus, about noon a great light from heaven suddenly shone around me. And I fell to the ground and heard a voice saying to me, 'Saul, Saul, why are you persecuting me?' And I answered, 'Who are you, Lord?' And he said to me, 'I am Jesus of Nazareth, whom you are persecuting.' Now those who were with me saw the light but did not understand the voice of the one who was speaking to me. And I said, 'What shall I do, Lord?' And the Lord said to me, 'Rise, and go into Damascus, and there you will be told all that is appointed for you to do.' And since I could not see because of the brightness of that light, I was led by the hand by those who were with me, and came into Damascus. And one Ananias, a devout man according to the law, well spoken of by all the Jews who lived there, came to me, and standing by me said to me, 'Brother Saul, receive your sight.' And at that very hour I received my sight and saw him. And he said, 'The God of our fathers appointed you to know his will, to see the Righteous One and to hear a voice from his mouth; for you will be a witness for him to everyone of what you have seen and heard. And now why do you wait? Rise and be baptized and wash away your sins, calling on his name.'"

What can be learned from Paul and how he shared his testimony in this context?

2. Augustine shared his own story but narrated the faith stories of others within that story. Is that applicable for evangelism today?

3. A number of early Christian evangelists crossed ideological frontiers and engaged intellectuals and heretics with the Gospel. What ideological frontiers must Christians cross today? What principles from the early Christian evangelists are useful today?

4. Patrick, Columba, and Julian first approached political leaders and gained permission to proclaim the Gospel. Is such an approach relevant for global evangelism today?

5

Bible Translation

In 1963, Dennis and Nancy Cochrane began serving as missionaries among the Duna people of Papua New Guinea. In order to adapt to living among this tribal people, it was imperative that they learn the language; although when they arrived in the region they did not speak a single word of Duna and their host people spoke no English. With no Duna alphabet, much less a place to take classes, the Cochranes persevered to gain proficiency in the language. Some words, such as "stick" and "rock," were quickly learned; however, it took the Cochranes nearly two years to discover a suitable dynamic equivalent for "faith." As skilled linguists serving with Wycliffe Bible translators, the Cochranes were eventually able to help the Duna develop a written language and translate Genesis, Mark, and other Scripture portions into the tribal language. Later, a complete Duna New Testament was completed.

As the people group began to read and study the Scriptures, the Cochranes observed that many of them believed the gospel and transformation was particularly evident in families as husbands began to treat their wives with love and tenderness. This testimony illustrates what Leslie Newbigin has written about the power of Scripture in mission: "But the introduction of the Bible changes the situation. It is not long before the Bible begins to make its own impact on its readers in the receptor community. In its stories, its prayers, its ethical teachings, and above all in the figure of Jesus as he presents himself to fresh eyes through the medium of print, the readers are confronted with something that raises questions both about their traditional culture and about what has been offered to them by the evangelist as 'Christianity.'"[1] After a decade, the Cochranes left Papua New Guinea due to health reasons; however, because the Duna had Scriptures in their language and a self-sustaining church, the Cochranes had effectively worked themselves out of a job.

This is just one account of the twentieth-century revolution in Bible translation that has occurred through the ministry of Wycliffe. The organization was founded in 1942 by William Cameron Townsend, "a missionary to the Cakchiquel Indians of Guatemala, [who] caught the vision for translation after Cakchiquel-speaking men expressed their concern and surprise that God did not speak their language."[2] With nearly 2,000 of the world's 6,800 language groups still without Scripture, organizations like Wycliffe labor to bring the Word of God to every cultural group in the world.[3] Though Wycliffe has been instrumental in accelerating the pace of Bible translation in the twentieth and twenty-first centuries, the value of translating Scripture was also evident in the early church. In fact, because the Gospels and New Testament were composed and circulated in common (koine) Greek, as opposed to Aramaic or even classical Greek, it can be argued that the New Testament Scriptures are translations in a sense and they testify to the missional nature of the faith.[4] Referring specifically to the four Gospels, Irvin and Sunquist have helpfully summarized, "Crucial for the transmission of this memory [of Jesus] was the composition of books we call Gospels."[5]

Lamin Sanneh, a leading scholar of global Christian history, has referred to this core value of the Christian faith—making Scripture available in the heart languages of the world's cultures—as the vernacular principle. Identifying Christianity as a "vernacular translation movement," Sanneh asserts that the "vintage mark" of the faith was that it has been a movement of "mission by translation."[6] Sanneh continues, "Mission as translation affirms the missio Dei [mission of God] as the hidden force for its work. It is the missio Dei that allowed translation to enlarge the boundaries of the

---

1. Newbigin, The Open Secret, 146–47.
2. "Wycliffe: Our History."
3. "Wycliffe: Translation Statistics."
4. Sanneh, Translating the Message, 1.
5. Irvin and Sunquist, History of the World Christian Movement, 50.
6. Sanneh, Translating the Message, 7, 29.

proclamation."[7] With the gospel moving across social and cultural bound-aries, Sanneh further adds that translating into local languages served to clarify the gospel message within a given people group. He writes, "Scriptural translation rested on the assumption that the vernacular has a primary affinity with the gospel, the point being conceded by the adoption of indigenous terms and concepts for the central categories of the Bible."[8] In short, Christian mission in the early church and later periods has been facilitated by Bible translation.[9]

In this chapter, we will explore evidence for the vernacular principle at work in the early church by narrating briefly some key accounts of Bible translation. Having already mentioned the significance of the *koine* Greek New Testament, we will focus on the translation of Scripture into Syriac, Latin, Coptic, Gothic, Armenian, Georgian, and Ethiopic in light of the church's missionary expansion in the first eight centuries.

Syriac

As shown, the Christian movement spread eastward in the second century from Antioch, the city where believers were first called Christians.[10] Led by the martyred bishop Ignatius, the church in Antioch was a Greek-speaking congregation. Yet, as Metzger notes, "though most of the mixed population of Antioch were acquainted with Greek, when the new faith spread elsewhere in Syria during the second half of the second century, the need was felt for a rendering of the Scriptures into the mother tongue of the populace."[11]

Irvin and Sunquist refer to Syriac as "a dialect of Aramaic that was closely related to Hebrew and originally spoken in the vicinity of Edessa."[12] Employing a different script from Aramaic or Hebrew, Syriac is defined simply by Black as the "ancient Semitic language and literature of the 'Syriac' Christians."[13] Black further highlights the significance of the region of Edessa and its language because it was the "only center of early Chris-

---

7. Ibid., 31, 82.

8. Ibid., 166.

9. See also Walls, *Missionary Movement*, 26–33.

10. Acts 11:26.

11. Metzger, *Bible in Translation*, 25–26.

12. Irvin and Sunquist, *History of the World Christian Movement*, 57.

13. Diringer, "Biblical Scripts," 24; also Metzger, *Bible in Translation*, 26.

tian life where the language of the Christian community was other than Greek."[14] According to Irvin and Sunquist, Syriac "became the language of choice among Christians in eastern Syria, Mesopotamia, Persia, and eventually India, Mongolia, and China."[15] The reason that the latter regions adopted Syriac was because it was the language of the Jacobite and Nestorian churches, the most active missional movements in the East throughout the early church period. Syriac and Latin were the first languages that Scripture was translated into; although scholars are divided over which translation occurred first.[16]

Probably, the initial efforts to translate Scripture into Syriac resulted in what is commonly known as the Old Syriac Scriptures. According to Metzger, much of the New Testament was available except for the General Epistles and Revelation, which the Syriac church apparently did not regard as canonical until the late third century.[17] However, the most celebrated early Syriac work of Scripture was Tatian's *Diatessaron*. Originally a musical term meaning "harmony," Tatian used it to describe his harmonized version of the four Gospels. Scholars are also divided over which translation developed first—the Old Syriac or the *Diatessaron*.[18] Also, some have asserted that Tatian first completed his work in Greek and then translated it to Syriac, while others argue that he was working uniquely in Syriac.[19] These questions aside, the point is that we begin to see Syriac Christians reading Scripture in their heart language in the late second and early third centuries. Paul Foster summarizes, "[Tatian's] combination of the four Gospels into a unified narrative was undoubtedly the most influential of such harmonies," and "his impact through the *Diatessaron* shaped Syriac Christianity for several centuries after his death."[20]

The Syriac Scriptures began to go through revision and development in the fourth century and the resulting text was known as the Peshitta,

---

14. Diringer, "Biblical Scripts," 26.

15. Irvin and Sunquist, *History of the World Christian Movement*, 57; also Diringer, "Biblical Scripts," 25–27.

16. Metzger, *Bible in Translation*, 25; also Birdsall, "New Testament Text," 346.

17. Metzger, *Bible in Translation*, 26; also Metzger, *Early Versions*, 44

18. Metzger, *Early Versions*, 3.

19. Foster, "Tatian," 23–27.

20. Foster, *Early Christian Thinkers*, xiii. For a more detailed analysis on the *Diatessaron*, see Metzger, *Early Versions*, 10–36; and Baarda, *Essays on the Diatessaron*.

which means "simple" or "clear."[21] Metzger writes that "this translation . . . was intended to supply a standardized version and to bring an end the confusion and variety of readings in earlier Syriac texts."[22] During the fourth century, the Old Testament began to be translated into Syriac for the first time though it is unclear whether the translators were Jews or Christian converts from Judaism with a working knowledge of Hebrew. In the same period, the Old Syriac New Testament went through significant revision.[23] The Syriac New Testament canon did grow during this time to twenty-two books as some of the General Epistles were accepted; however, 2 Peter, 2 and 3 John, and Revelation were still not considered canonical. However, when the Syrian Jacobite church revised the New Testament in the sixth century, they concurred with the view of the broader catholic church and accepted all twenty-seven New Testament books. [24] Finally, the Peshitta Scriptures—including both the Old and New Testaments—went through further revision in the seventh century.[25]

In the first six centuries, the Syriac speaking Christians possessed as many as six different translations of the Old and New Testaments.[26] While this has presented a challenge to textual critics to make sense of what the Syrian Christians were reading, what is apparent is that the Syriac church clearly valued the central role of Scripture in its worship and discipleship as it expanded in the East. The efforts to develop and revise the Peshitta in particular also demonstrate the missional value of clarifying the Scriptures and rendering a high level of understanding in the Syriac vernacular. Finally, while the Syriac Bible was arguably the earliest translation of Scripture in the early church, the Syriac Scripture project later influenced the translation structure of the Armenian, Georgian, and Arabic Scriptures.[27]

Latin — WESTERN CHURCH

Though the translation of the Scriptures into Latin was one of the earliest in church history and probably occurred in the late second or early third

21. Margolis, *Story of Bible Translations*, 45; also Metzger, *Early Versions*, 48.

22. Metzger, *Early Versions*, 3.

23. Ibid., 27–28.

24. Ibid., 28

25. Ibid., 28–29; cf. Jenkings, *Lost History*, 86–88.

26. Metzger, *Early Versions*, 3.

27. Metzger, *Bible in Translation*, 29.

century, the precise origins of the Old Latin Bible are unknown. As the church at Rome was continuing to use the Greek Bible in worship until the mid-third century, the Old Latin Bible was probably developed in North Africa.[28]

One of the fascinating and troubling aspects of the early Latin Bible is the abundance of variant readings that are available. There was not a single translator or team of translators and African fathers such as Tertullian and Cyprian seemed to use diverse language to render some passages of Scripture. In addition, the Old Testament was largely based on the Greek Septuagint, an issue that would be later addressed in Jerome's work on the Latin Vulgate. While the variant readings may seem problematic to the modern reader, the reality is that the Latin Bible project, like the Syriac Scriptures, was driven by worship and discipleship. That is, in worship assemblies in the late second century African church, the Greek Scriptures were read while a simultaneous line-by-line translation into Latin probably followed facilitating understanding in the vernacular.[29] As these translations were captured in writing and as further revisions occurred, the Old Latin Bible became a "living creation, constantly growing."[30]

Eventually, the Old Latin Bible could be identified through three regional streams: the African, as evidenced in Cyprian's preaching; the Gallic, observed in Irenaeus; and the Italian, which was used by Augustine.[31] Despite the diversity in vocabulary used in these Latin Bibles, Margolis asserts that there is still much continuity in these Scriptures due to the vernacular principle. He writes, "What is common to all of [the translations] is the character of the Latin, which is not the classical but of the rustic variety such as was used in popular speech throughout the confines of the empire."[32] His additional comments also speak to the missional nature of the Latin Scriptures: "The new religion—Christianity—had been embraced by the humble and poor, the scriptural message was for the people, the broad masses, and it was fitting that the Bible everywhere should fit their language."[33]

28. Metzger, *Early Versions*, 288.

29. Ibid., 286; also Metzger, *Bible in Translation,* 30; and Birdsall, "New Testament Text," 338, 346.

30. Metzger, *Bible in Translation,* 30.

31. Metzger, *Early Versions*, 327–30; also Metzger, *Bible in Translation,* 31.

32. Margolis, *Story of Bible Translations*, 46.

33. Ibid.

While the Latin speaking church was clearly local and reflected the regional expressions of the Western Roman Empire, the lack of a universally recognized Latin Bible was the source of frustration for church fathers such as Augustine. In his *Teaching Christianity*, a manual on teaching the Bible and the Christian faith, Augustine complained: "Those who translated the Scriptures from Hebrew into Greek can be counted; this is certainly not true of Latin translators. The fact is that whenever in the early days of the faith a Greek codex came into anybody's hands, and he felt he had the slightest familiarity with each language, he rushed in with translation."[34]

Figure 6: Facsimile of the Book of Kells at Iona.

Augustine's concerns about the variant readings of the Old Latin Bible were shared by Bishop Damasus of Rome who challenged Jerome (ca. 347–420) with the task of revising the Latin Gospels, a project that would ultimately result in the Latin Vulgate. Jerome was a monk who had mastered classical Latin in his youth and later gained proficiency in Greek. In addition, after studying some Hebrew in Rome, he incorporated Hebrew study into his monastic withdrawal—an ascetic discipline that helped him

34. Augustine, *Teaching Christianity* 2.11.16 (WSA).

to deal with the temptations of the flesh. As a result, Jerome was just one of a handful of church fathers—including Origen, Ephraim the Syrian, and Epiphanias—who possessed any skills in the Hebrew language. Given his linguistic abilities, Jerome was by far the best candidate to undertake a significant revision of the Old Latin Bible.[35]

Though initially reluctant to take on the project because of the negative reactions he anticipated facing from Latin speaking church leaders and Christians, Jerome ultimately accepted Damasus's challenge and began working on the Gospels revision around 383 and completed them in just two years. Next, he began revising Paul's letters, the Psalms and Job. Finally, between 389 and 405, he turned his focus to doing a fresh translation of the entire Old Testament. Convinced of the value of Hebrew verity, Jerome's greatest innovation in translation came when he insisted on translating the Old Testament directly from Hebrew into Latin.[36] In this way, he broke with the practice of the Old Latin Bible translators who based their translations on the Greek Septuagint because the prevailing view—one held by Augustine—was that the Septuagint itself was inspired. Hence, Jerome's work moved from being a mere revision of the Old Latin to a new and fresh translation for the fifth-century Latin-speaking church.

When the Vulgate was published and began to be circulated around the Roman world in the early fifth century, there was some negative backlash—precisely what Jerome had feared. The most famous incident, related by Augustine in his *Letter 71* to Jerome, occurred during a church service in the North African city of Oea (modern Tripoli). When the lector arrived at Jonah 4:6 in the Scripture reading (regarding the plant that God made grow to offer Jonah shade), the congregation reacted violently when they hear that "gourd" (*cucurbita*) from the Old Latin Bible had been replaced by "ivy" (*hedera*) in the new translation. The riot continued until the reader was forced to revert back to the familiar reading. While this account might reinforce a stereotype that church people are traditional, resistant to change, and perhaps looking for a reason to fight, there is some missional significance. Despite the noted variant readings in the Old Latin Bible, this assembly of believers clearly had convictions about the accuracy of Scripture. As the Word of God was life-giving to this believing community— a guide for worship and discipleship—it could not be altered or defiled. In this sense, the church at Oea's regard for Scripture was not terribly

35. Metzger, *Bible in Translation*, 32.

36. Metzger, *Early Versions*, 333.

unlike that of Damasus or Jerome. The remarkable difference is that this congregation was probably made up of oral learners—those who prefer to communicate through speaking and listening rather than writing. Hence, on account of their robust oral memories, they recognized the changes in Jonah 4 when the Scriptures were chanted in the worship assembly. Finally, this congregation was also not that different from Augustine whose sermons and writings were so saturated with references to the Old Latin Scriptures that Harmless concluded that Augustine "spoke Bible, making its words his words."[37]

What was the legacy of Jerome and the Latin Vulgate? Though the Vulgate did not find full acceptance in Jerome's lifetime, it would ultimately serve as a catalyst for Latin becoming the predominant language of worship in the western church, including regions like Roman Britain. Metzger writes, "For nearly a thousand years, the Vulgate was used as the recognized text of Scripture throughout Western Europe."[38] Discussing the Vulgate's impact on western doctrine, Metzger adds, "The theology and the devotional language typical of the Roman Catholic Church were either created or transmitted by the Vulgate."[39] This included theological terms such as justification, regeneration, and sanctification that were eventually translated into English.[40] The widespread acceptance of the Vulgate in the western church within a developing paradigm of medieval Christendom surely stifled Bible vernacular translations during this period. However, Metzger helpfully notes that the Vulgate "became the basis for the pre-Reformation vernacular Scriptures, such as Wycliffe's English translation in the fourteenth century, as well as the first printed Bibles in German (1466), Italian (1471), Catalán (1478), Czech (1488), and French (1530)."[41] In short, Jerome's fourth and fifth century work proved useful once conviction for vernacular Scriptures was rekindled around the time of the Protestant Reformation.

LATIN - WESTERN CHURCH

37. Harmless, *Augustine in His Own Words*, 156.
38. Metzger, *Bible in Translation*, 35.
39. Ibid., 32
40. Ibid., 30.
41. Ibid., 35.

The Vernacular Principle and Vatican II

"Easy access to Sacred Scripture should be provided for all the Christian faithful . . . since the word of God should be accessible at all times, the church by her authority and with maternal concern sees to it that suitable and correct translations are made into different languages, especially from the original texts of the sacred books."[42] These words, from Pope Paul VI's letter *Verbum Dei*, represent one of the significant outcomes of the Second Vatican Council, which convened from 1962 to 1965. After more than a millennium of elevating the stature and function of the Latin Vulgate Bible in worship and teaching, it seems that the Roman Catholic Church accepted a paradigm shift and embraced the vernacular principle. This value has also been observed in the ecumenical dialogues of Pope Benedict XVI.[43]

Coptic — EGYPT

While Greek was the primary language of Egypt's Hellenized urban centers, Coptic was widely spoken in towns and villages in the early church period. Despite Black's reference to Coptic as the "the non-cultivated speech of Egypt,"[44] it was arguably the heart language of Athanasius, the Alexandrian bishop and a key contributor to fourth-century Trinitarian theology.[45]

When the Coptic alphabet was developed, it included twenty-four Greek letters and seven other symbols. Noting the interesting origins of the new alphabet, Plumely writes: "When Christianity came into Egypt, a long-established system of writing was still in use, but the propagators of the new faith decided that a new form of writing should be used for the purposes of evangelism. The old system of writing, though capable of expressing the new truth, was both far too intricate and too gravely contaminated by its content of many symbolic forms redolent of an ancient and discredited paganism."[46] Thus, it seems fair to argue that the Coptic language came into being because of mission and the motivation to distinguish a Christian worldview from the prevailing Egyptian pagan worldview. In addition, the Coptic literature that emerged in the first five centuries, which included

42. Pope Paul VI, *Dei Verbum*, 6.22.
43. Moon, "Why Evangelical Leaders Love Pope Benedict XVI."
44. Black, "Biblical Scripts," 27.
45. Metzger, *Early Versions*, 105–7.
46. Cited in ibid., 142.

Scripture, liturgy, and a body of sacred biographies, was dominated by a Christian worldview.[47]

Due to the dispersion of Coptic peoples along the Nile River, six Coptic dialects emerged: Sahidic, Bohairic, Achmimic, sub-Achmimic, Middle Egyptian (Oxyrhnchite), and Fayyumic.[48] Metzger argues that Bible translation into the Coptic dialects began in the third and fourth centuries; however, Black suggests that translation efforts were initiated in Sahidic and Bohairic in the second and third centuries.[49] Kasser, agreeing with Black, asserts that preliminary translations began as early as the mid-second century in what he describes as "ad hoc oral translations of individual passages . . . made for liturgical use."[50] Not unlike the development of the Old Latin Bible, the need for Coptic Scriptures was driven by liturgical and discipleship needs—certainly the fruit of mission. Also similar to the Latin and Syriac Scriptures, the Coptic Bible became more formalized as the Egyptian church grew and desired a clearer and more official translation.[51] Eventually, the Bohairic dialect became the standard version for the Coptic Church.

Evaluating the legacy of the Coptic Scriptures, Metzger writes: "The [Bohairic] version ultimately became the accepted Bible in Egypt, and the dialect survived as the ecclesiastical and liturgical language of the Coptic Church, even after Arabic had been adopted as the speech of everyday life."[52] Similarly, Ward adds: "The Bible and liturgy had been translated into Coptic languages. They, along with monasticism, became the principle vehicle for the survival of Christianity in an increasingly Arabic and Islamic culture."[53] Finally, more than being a mere means of survival for Coptic Christianity, the Coptic Scriptures also influenced the religious life of at least one other Egyptian people group as the Nubian peoples adopted Coptic as their official language of worship.[54]

---

47. Metzger, *Bible in Translation,* 35; also Diringer, "Biblical Scripts," 27.

48. Metzger, *Bible in Translation,* 36.

49. Ibid., 36; also Birdsall, "New Testament Text," 347; and Diringer, "Biblical Scripts," 27.

50. Cited in Metzger, *Early Versions,* 129.

51. Ibid., 129–32.

52. Metzger, *Bible in Translation,* 36–37.

53. Ward, "Africa," 195.

54. Diringer, "Biblical Scripts," 28.

Gothic ~~Europe~~

The Goths were a Germanic people that originated from north of the Danube River. Eventually, they divided into two distinct groups: the Visigoths or western Goths and the Ostrogoths who lived in the East in what is now Hungary. While the Ostrogoths enjoyed a peaceful relationship with the eastern Roman Empire at Constantinople; the Visigoths are remembered in history for sacking the city of Rome in the early fifth century and then taking control of much of the western empire, including North Africa.[55]

The Visigoths were probably first exposed to Christians upon their expansion into Moesia and Dacia (modern Romania and Bulgaria); however, the most celebrated missionary to them was Ulfilas. Half Gothic and half Cappadocian, Ulfilas grew up around Constantinople. In 340, he was consecrated as bishop to the Goths by Eusebius of Nicomedia, the moderate Arian bishop who had baptized Constantine toward the end of the emperor's life. As shown, Ulfilas shared Eusebius' moderate Arian theology.

In addition to being a missionary-bishop to the Visigoths, Ulfilas labored to make Scripture available in the Gothic language. As the vernacular was unwritten, he began by developing an alphabet from a combination of Greek, Latin, and ancient Germanic letters. According to Metzger, Ulfilas' translation methodology was word-for-word, which resulted in a rather wooden translation.[56] Another interesting element in Ulfilas' approach was that he purposefully omitted Kings and Samuel from the Gothic Old Testament because he feared that the Visigoths, who were already known for their warring ways, would be more given to warfare from reading these books of Scripture.[57]

Due to the Visigoth's fifth-century conquest of the western Roman Empire, Gothic became widely spoken in what is now Europe, which should have afforded the Gothic Bible to influence the spread of Christianity in the region. However, with the Byzantine resurgence in the following century, the Gothic language largely died out as a vernacular.[58] Among the few surviving manuscripts, the most famous is the Codex Argenteus ("silver"), a collection of the four Gospels, which dates to the sixth century. Fitting its description, this book was fabricated by printing silver letters onto a purple

---

55. Metzger, *Bible in Translation*, 38.

56. Metzger, *Early Versions*, 382–84.

57. Metzger, *Bible in Translation*, 38–39.

58. Metzger, *Early Versions*, 377–78.

parchment. Another interesting element of the codex was the ordering of the Gospels—Matthew, John, Luke, and Mark—which was probably an indication of which apostles were most important to the Gothic church.[59] Despite the uniqueness of the Codex Argenteus, the Gothic Scriptures had virtually no effect on the church in the region after the sixth century.

Armenian

As discussed, Armenia was evangelized in the late third century by Gregory the Enlightener. After King Tiridates was reached with the gospel and baptized, he declared Armenia to be a Christian nation around 301.[60]

Bible Translation for Oral Learners

The response of the church at Oea to the language of the Latin Vulgate (Augustine's *Letter* 71 to Jerome) is in part an indication that this community was comprised of many oral learners. To their credit, oral learners seem to have a robust memory and the capacity to retain large passages of Scripture. Yet, how do we approach Bible translation for those who cannot read or do not prefer to receive vital information through print means? Should the product of Bible translation always be a printed book and should oral learners be required to read in order to access Scripture? As the issue of making disciples of oral learners has become a priority for a number of missions organizations and groups, this has also affected strategies in Bible translation.[61] In addition to continuing to produce printed Scriptures, Wycliffe, in partnership with other organizations, is increasingly developing oral versions of Scripture in which oral learners can hear the Bible on CD and other audio devices. They can also view Bible stories on video. Finally, these strategies have been accompanied by a new generation of missionaries and national Christians capable of relating the Bible chronologically and through story form.

The primary spiritual influences on Armenia came from Syria as the Bible and Christian literature were available in Greek and Syriac—a spiritual benefit to Armenians with proficiency in those languages. The need

59. Metzger, *Bible in Translation*, 39.

60. Agathangelos, *History of the Armenians*, in Coakley and Sterk, eds., *Readings in World Christian History*, 122–30.

61. See Willis et al., "Making Disciples of Oral Leaners" and the work of groups like International Orality Network and Orality Strategies (International Mission Board, Southern Baptist Convention).

for Scripture in the Armenian language was first recognized by a certain Bishop Daniel who was a native of Syria. As the Armenian language did not exist in written form, the bishop attempted to develop an alphabet by borrowing letters from Aramaic. Though Daniel clearly exhibited missional concerns for the Armenian people through his efforts, this initial attempt to develop the Armenian alphabet ultimately failed.[62]

In the early fifth century, the vision for the Armenian Scriptures was revived through Sahak, the leader of the Armenian church. Irvin and Sunquist write, "The patriarch Sahak (d. 439) assisted by a scribe named Mashtots (or Mesrop) (362–440), set to work to create a new alphabet for the language."[63] Apparently, Persian advisers were invited into the process of developing the Armenian script. Metzger adds that "Mesrop gathered about him a band of keen scholars. Sending some of them to Edessa, to Constantinople, and as far as Rome in search of manuscripts of the Scriptures and of ecclesiastical and secular writers, he inaugurated a program of translation which enriched and consolidated the Armenian culture."[64]

Beginning the project around 406, Mesrop seemed to work efficiently as the New Testament was completed by 410, while the Old Testament translation was finished by 414. Scholars remain divided over whether the Armenians worked from the Syriac or Greek Bibles as a basis for their translation.[65] Interestingly, the first Old Testament book that they translated was Proverbs, which probably reveals some affinity that the Armenian church had for the wisdom literature of the Bible. Further, the Armenian Bible also included some Old and New Testament apocryphal books that were rejected as non-canonical by the broader church.[66] Finally, Irvin and Sunquist note that in addition to translating the Scriptures into Armenian, Mesrop and his colleagues also contributed a "large body of liturgical and theological books into their native tongue."[67]

---

62. Metzger, *Bible in Translation*, 41; cf. Wilken, *First Thousand Years*, 231.

63. Irvin and Sunquist, *History of the World Christian Movement*, 206.

64. Metzger, *Early Translations*, 156.

65. Ibid., 164–65.

66. Metzger, *Bible in Translation*, 41–42.

67. Irvin and Sunquist, *History of the World Christian Movement*, 206.

Georgian

According to church tradition, the people of Georgia were evangelized during the reign of Constantine. Scholars seem to agree and the consensus is that there was a Christian presence in the region by the mid-fourth century.[68] Armenian church tradition claims that the initiative to evangelize and translate the Scriptures for the Georgian people came from Armenia. Metzger writes, "After St. Mesrop had drawn up an alphabet for his fellow countrymen, he became concerned about the lack of alphabet among the neighboring Georgian people. After he had invented an alphabet that represented the sounds that occur in that language, King Bakur of Georgia arranged that it should be taught to boys of the lower social classes at various districts and provinces."[69] Though it is disputed whether the Georgian Scriptures were translated from Armenian, Syriac, or Greek, most scholars affirm that the Gospels and parts of the New Testament were available in Georgian by the fifth century.[70] In summary, the Georgian Scriptures were available within a century of Christianity's arrival in the region and it is possible that it resulted as part of the Armenian church's mission.

Ethiopic (Ge'ez)

As discussed, the most accelerated mission activity in Ethiopia began in the fourth century after Aedesius and Frumentius were shipwrecked in Aksum and later gained favor to preach. In 341, Frumentius traveled to Alexandria where he was set apart as a missionary bishop for Ethiopia by Athanasius.

According to Metzger, the origins of the Ethiopic (also called Ge'ez) alphabet are probably traced to the South Semitic or Sabaen alphabet from Yemen. In the first half of the fourth century, following Frumentius and Aedesius' mission, the Ethiopic alphabet was fully developed. Comprised of twenty-six letters, Ethiopic read from left to right, which distinguished it from other Semitic languages.[71]

The question of when the Bible became available in Ethiopic is disputed. Metzger argues that translation began in the fifth or sixth century, while Irvin and Sunquist claim that it was part of Frumentius' fourth-century

---

68. Metzger, *Bible in Translation*, 43.

69. Ibid.

70. Ibid.; also Hastings, *World History of Christianity*, 30.

71. Metzger, *Early Versions*, 216.

mission work.[72] Despite this disagreement, it is affirmed that the Ethiopic Old Testament was translated from the Septuagint and it appears that the translators were unaware of or unmoved by Jerome's values of Hebrew verity. One interesting fact is that the Ethiopic Bible contained eighty-one books—nine additional apocryphal books that were rejected by the western catholic church.[73] In terms of its legacy, although Amharic is the national language of modern Ethiopia, Ethiopic remains the Scriptural and liturgical language of the contemporary Ethiopian Orthodox Church.

Conclusion

It is evident from this brief summary of these language groups, that the early church valued the vernacular principle. Given this general assertion, what conclusions can be made about Bible translation in the period of our study? First, unlike the work of Wycliffe and others today, in the early church, Bible translation seemed to follow mission expansion and the establishment of churches. We have observed that, initially, many churches worshipped in a regional trade language and many Christians who were fluent in another language benefited from Scripture or Christian literature through that medium. However, in each case discussed, the vernacular principle prevailed and Scripture was made available in many of the heart languages of peoples where the gospel had taken hold. In this sense, Irvin and Sunquist are correct to conclude that "translocation [of the gospel message] and translation went hand in hand."[74]

Second, worship seems to have driven the process of Bible translation. As the gospel spread and as new communities of believers sprang up, it was imperative that Scripture—what Athanasius called the "springs of salvation"[75]—be read publicly as a focal point of worship assemblies. As noted, the Latin Bible was developed in the African context as it was translated simultaneously while the Greek Scriptures were being read aloud. Though this led to the challenge of variant readings, we must conclude

72. Metzger, *Bible in Translation*, 45; also Irvin and Sunquist, *History of the World Christian Movement*, 217–18.

73. Irvin and Sunquist, *History of the World Christian Movement*, 217–18; also Diringer, "Biblical Scripts," 28.

74. Irvin and Sunquist, *History of the World Christian Movement*, 54.

75. Athanasius, *Letter* 39 (NPNF 2:4).

that this was a worshipping church that was demanding Scripture in the vernacular.

Third, while the need for Scripture in worship assemblies had been a catalyst for initial translations, concerns for discipleship drove the process of revising those works. The Peshitta Syriac, Latin Vulgate, and later editions of Scripture in other languages certainly show that the early church was concerned about the accuracy of Scripture. This desire for accurate Scripture also points to another early Christian value—sound doctrine—that was held by the early church and characterized the ministries of Athanasius, the Cappadocians, and Augustine among others.[76]

Fourth, it would be helpful to discuss briefly the legacy of Bible translation in the early Christian period. On a positive note, communities that translated Scripture into the local vernacular managed to avoid extinction, especially following the rise of Islam in the seventh century. The Coptic and Ethiopic Scriptures seem to have played a key role in sustaining the churches of Egypt and Ethiopia even after Christianity became a minority religion.[77] On the contrary, Sanneh correctly notes, "The failure to produce a Punic version of the Bible was an ill omen for the church in North Africa, for it left indigenous populations excluded from any meaningful role in Christianity."[78] The fact that the church was limited to Latin Scriptures helps explain why the church in North Africa went from being one of the fastest growing churches in the Roman period to virtually non-existent once the Arabs took control of the region.[79]

A final point of Bible translation legacy worth noting is the irony of the Latin Vulgate. Commissioned in the fourth century to clarify the Scriptures for Latin-speaking Christians and to serve as a vernacular translation, by the seventh century, the western church had elevated the Vulgate as the standard Bible for the global church. Having becoming a symbol of western religious hegemony, the Vulgate's presence effectively stifled vernacular translation efforts until the fifteenth century.[80]

---

76. See my discussion in Smither, *Augustine as Mentor,* 9, 11, 19–20, 38, 51–52, 69, 87, 104, 238–44.

77. Regarding Coptic and Egypt, see Wilken, *First Thousand Years,* 319.

78. Sanneh, *Translating the Message,* 69.

79. Decret, *Early Christianity in North Africa,* 198–201; also Wilken, *First Thousand Years,* 320.

80. Sanneh, *Translating the Message,* 73–76.

In summary, in this chapter, it has been argued that a key element of early Christian mission was making Scripture available in the heart languages of the peoples where the church had been established. Though the narrative of Bible translation history is marked by struggle and disagreement, there is no question that Scripture was central to church life in early Christian history. Today, with over 1,900 of the world's languages still without the Bible, the translation work initiated in the early Christian period is far from over.

Questions for Reflection

1. Read 2 Tim 3:14-17:

   But as for you, continue in what you have learned and have firmly believed, knowing from whom you learned it and how from childhood you have been acquainted with the sacred writings, which are able to make you wise for salvation through faith in Christ Jesus. All Scripture is breathed out by God and profitable for teaching, for reproof, for correction, and for training in righteousness, that the man of God may be complete, equipped for every good work.

   In the early church, the Bible was needed to facilitate worship and teaching? Do you see the missional purpose of Scripture in your local congregation?

2. The early church was concerned about revising Scripture for the sake of accuracy and sound doctrine. How would that value help the church today?

3. What lessons can be learned from the failure to translate Scripture into the Punic language of North Africa?

4. What lessons can be learned from the Latin Vulgate becoming so prized in medieval Europe by non-Latin speakers?

5. Presently there are still more than 1,900 language groups in the world without a word of Scripture in their language? How should we feel about this? How can we tangibly act?

6

Contextualization

In an article entitled "Behold the Ox of God," Joy Anderson related some of her story serving as a Bible translator among the Dinka people of southern Sudan. As she and her husband struggled to understand and probe the culture, they discovered some intriguing aspects of Dinka culture that offered some apparent effective bridges to communicating the gospel. For instance, regarding the Dinka views on sacrifice, she related:

> The Dinkas seek to restore their broken relationship with God through a system of sacrifice similar to that of the ancient Hebrews . . . their generic term for sacrifice is ox, but the sacrifice can at times include the wild cucumber as well as other animals . . . "It is one's bull that redeems him," goes a Dinka song. The New Testament talks of Jesus' sacrifice taking the place of animal sacrifices. The book of Hebrews shows that, while the sacrifice of bulls cannot once and for all take away our sin, the blood of Jesus Christ can (Heb. 10:1–10). What a wonderful answer we have for the Dinka, to agree with them that a sacrifice is necessary, and that Jesus has provided the perfect sacrifice. Jesus, indeed, is the "Ox of God."[1]

Such an account illustrates not only a bridge to gospel communication but also the idigenizing principle articulated by historian of mission Andrew Walls. That is, in Wall's words, because of the model of Christ's incarnation, the gospel ought to be at home in every culture. If the good

1. Anderson, "Behold the Ox of God."

news is a seed, then it should germinate, take root, and flower in the soils of the world's cultures. On the other hand, Walls asserts that the gospel is also a pilgrim message and foreign to each culture because of the devastating impact of the fall on individuals and societies. So in receiving the gospel, individuals, families, and people groups must also renounce and turn from personal and social sins.[2] In short, as the gospel is at the same time at home and pilgrim, it becomes a welcome offense to the nations that receive it.

The process of navigating the complexity of communicating the gospel among the people groups of the world is known today as contextualization. Showing great concern for the integrity of the biblical gospel while making the message relevant and understood in a given host culture, David Hesselgrave defines contextualization as "the attempt to communicate the message of the person, works, Word, and will of God in a way that is faithful to God's revelation, especially as it is put forth in the teachings of the Holy Scriptures, and that it is meaningful to respondents in their respective cultural and existential contexts."[3] With simple precision, Nigerian theologian Josphat Yego adds that contextualization "means the never-changing Word of God in ever-changing modes of relevance. It is making the gospel concepts or ideals relevant in a given situation."[4] I would qualify that contextualization should not be construed as adapting the gospel as much as it is clarifying the unchanging message for the cultures and people groups of the world.

Do we see evidence of contextualization in the early church? In the concluding chapter of his work *The First Thousand Years*, Robert Wilken, a ranking scholar in early Christian studies, insightfully wrote: "The adaptability of Christianity to diverse linguistic and cultural traditions is remarkable. Christianity brought something new and at the same time received something old."[5] It seems that Wilken is asserting that a key element of Christianity's success in quickly becoming a global faith was due to the movement's inherent contextual nature. In reality, two previous chapters in the present work—those on evangelism and Bible translation—have already testified to Christianity's contextual concerns. While the process of making the Scriptures clear through vernacular translation and proclaim-

2. Walls, *Missionary Movement*, 7–9.

3. Hesselgrave, "Contextualization that is Authentic and Relevant," 115.

4. Cited in Moreau, *Contextualization in World Missions,* 35.

5. Wilken, *First Thousand Years,* 356.

ing the gospel as the church moved across geographical, linguistic, and cultural boundaries in the early centuries does imply a level of contextualization, the present chapter will explore more closely how contextualization occurred. Specifically, we will consider how **(1)** Christian missionaries articulated the faith through commonly understood ideas, **(2)** engaging sacred space, **(3)** through visual and work culture. Finally, this chapter will also briefly highlight how the church failed at points to be indigenous in its message and approach.

(1) Ideas and Forms

As discussed in the evangelism chapter, some early Christian missionaries were also philosophers who were quite conversant with the worldview and ideas of their age. This was particularly true as the church expanded and grew within the Greek-speaking and thinking world. Walls writes, "The dominant expression of Christian faith for several centuries resulted from its steady penetration of Hellenistic thought and culture during a period when that culture was also associated with a single political entity, the Roman Empire."[6] One of the realities of the Hellenistic world was that there was a precise system of thought and the gospel was thought about and later theologized in this context.[7]

As shown, the Greek apologists, led by Justin, proved capable of relating to and communicating Christian thought in this Hellenistic milieu. Origen was also well versed in Platonic philosophy and used that framework to clarify the gospel to the likes of Celsus.[8]

One specific example worth noting is Justin's choice to communicate Jesus as the Word of God by employing the Greek word *Logos*.[9] As *Logos* was common vocabulary that expressed at least the Stoic notion of God, Sara Parvis suggests that "through this concept of *Logos*, Justin was building bridges" to the broader culture.[10] Commenting further on his motivations and his own epistemological assumptions, Parvis adds that Justin "found a

6. Walls, *Missionary Movement*, 18.

7. Ibid., 18–19.

8. Wilken, *First Thousand Years*, 55, 63.

9. Irvin and Sunquist, *History of the World Christian Movement*, 55; Parvis, "Justin Martyr," 9–10.

10. Parvis, "Justin Martyr," 10.

way of engaging with the outside world, driven by the deep conviction that there was a common universe of discourse accessible to all human beings."[11]

While Justin contextualized biblical ideas in the building material of Hellenistic culture, it also appears that he borrowed at least one form of Roman communication to make his point. Justin is particularly remembered for his *First Apology* in which he defended the church against the charges of atheism and cannibalism among other things, while also clarifying what Christians believed and how they worshipped. What the modern reader may perhaps miss is that this apologetic genre of writing was not Justin's innovation. Rather, as Parvis shows, he employed an accepted form of petition from the Roman court system known as the *biblidion* (later *libellus* in Latin) to make his case. Parvis asserts, "What Justin did was to hijack this normal Roman administrative procedure and turn it into a vehicle for articulating and disseminating the message of the gospel" and, in turn, he "turned a petition into an apology."[12] In short, Justin was not only conversant with the worldview of his Hellenistic context but he also understood the medium of Roman legal communication in order to get a hearing for his case. Justin's apologetic form was clearly influential and employed by others as his disciples Athenagoras and Tatian adopted his approach in the Greek speaking world, while Tertullian made use of it in his African Latin context.[13]

Justin's legacy continues through the fifth century as Augustine wrote *The City of God*—his magnum opus that thoroughly responded to the pagan allegations that Christians were to blame for the fall of Rome. Describing his aims in a letter to a friend, Augustine writes: "There are twenty-two books . . . in the first ten, the vanities of the impious have been refuted, and in the other twelve, our religion has been described and defended."[14] Though Augustine wrote in order to equip Christians to defend their faith in a pagan context, he also intended that *The City of God* would actually be read by pagans themselves.[15] William Harmless concludes, "This massive work stands in a centuries-long tradition of Christian apologetics,

---

11. Ibid., 12.

12. Ibid., 6–7.

13. Ibid., 13; Foster, "Tatian," 19.

14. Augustine, *Letter* 1*A (Divjak), cited in Harmless, *Augustine in His Own Words*, 326.

15. Ibid., 327.

pioneered by Justin Martyr and Athenagoras . . . Augustine's work has been called the finest Christian apology of antiquity."[16]

Outside of Rome and the Hellenistic world, an effort to contextualize through accepted ideas and forms can also be observed in the work of Nestorian missionaries in China. As Alopen and his monks made favorable contact with the Chinese emperor between 635 and 638, one of their mission strategies was to develop a Chinese Christian literature. An early form of this was a work that included four treatises devoted to Jesus, God's nature, creation and human nature, and on Christ's ethical teachings. This medium seems deliberately contextual because the four texts were clearly patterned after the Buddhist genre of sutras. Within this literary form, the Nestorians went even farther and use the term "Buddha" to refer to divinity. Also, they chose to use a very local Chinese term for God while referring to the Holy Spirit as the "pure wind." As the challenge of finding a suitable equivalent for God's name in Chinese would continue to perplex missionaries through the twentieth century, the early Nestorian decision in this area is significant. Nestorian missionaries also seemed to be contextualizing in the Buddhist context when they constructed stone crosses—a clear text of material culture. Regarding this, Jenkins writes, "one moving visual token of the Nestorians' effort to make their faith intelligible is the combined lotus-cross symbol that appears widely . . . on tombstones from China's Fujian Province."[17] Finally, Nestorian monasticism itself, which resembled Buddhist asceticism at least to some extent, also seemed to connect with the host culture.

Despite these clear efforts to contextualize the gospel in China, it could be argued that the Nestorians overly identified with Chinese Buddhism for when China later came under Taoist leadership, Christianity was regarded as a foreign religion. Despite the work to develop a Chinese Christian literature, one clear shortcoming was that the Nestorians failed to translate the Scriptures into Chinese.[18] Finally, the case could be made that the Nestorians went beyond merely clarifying the gospel in China and promoted a syncretistic form of Christianity that was mixed with Buddhism.

16. Ibid., 316.

17. Jenkins, *Lost History of Christianity*, 92.

18. Irvin and Sunquist, *History of the World Christian Movement*, 317–22; cf. Jenkins, *Lost History of Christianity*, 15–16, 64.

Sacred Space and Festivals

Alan Kreider has asserted that one of the outcomes of Rome's Christian-ization—not necessarily its transformation through mission—was that Roman society's symbols, art, and rituals began to be Christian.[19] This was expressed concretely in a number of contexts through the "baptizing" of public spaces. This included removing architecture and symbols that paid any homage to pagan belief and replacing them with Christian symbols. Leithart argues that Constantine's plans for constructing of the new Rome at Constantinople—particularly the city's forum—was driven by this value.[20] In the late fourth and early fifth centuries, following the Emperor Theodosius' declaration that Christianity was the imperial religion, Bish-ops Theophilus of Alexandria and Synesius of Cyrene waged a campaign to cleanse the public spaces of their cities from pagan idolatry.[21] Describing the process in Alexandria, the church historian Socrates stated that "the images of their [pagan] gods [were] molten into pots and other convenient utensils for the use of the Alexandrian church."[22] In short, following Constantine, baptizing public spaces implied the imperial suppression of paganism, which came to a climax in 529 with Justinian's legislation to close the last pagan temples.[23] Despite such actions, Ramsay MacMullen has made a com-pelling case that paganism remained alive and well in the region through the eighth century.[24]

Given this tendency within Rome to baptize public areas by removing or destroying pagan sacred space, let us consider an alternative and argu-ably contextual approach to addressing non-Christian sacred space in Au-gustine of Canterbury's late sixth-century mission to England. As shown, Augustine and a team of monks were sent by Bishop Gregory to evangelize the Anglo people. The correspondence between Augustine and Gregory regarding the mission has been preserved in Bede's *Ecclesiastical History of the English People*. One of the issues that Augustine raised was what to do about the presence of pagan temples in the region, especially as the English began to convert. Clearly breaking with the imperial policy of demolish-ing such structures, Gregory advised Augustine: "The idol temples of that

19. Kreider, *Change of Conversion*, 91–98.

20. Leithart, *Defending Constantine*, 303, 326–33.

21. Oden, *Early Libyan Christianity*, 180.

22. Cited in ibid.

23. Kreider, *Change of Conversion*, 39.

24. MacMullen, *Christianity and Paganism*, 34–36, 41.

[English] race should by no means be destroyed, but only the idols in them . . . For if the shrines are well built, it is essential that they should be changed from the worship of devils to the service of the true God. When this people see that their shrines are not destroyed they will be able to banish error from their hearts and be more ready to come to the places they are familiar with, but now recognizing and worshipping the true God."[25] While Gregory was clearly intolerant of the continued presence of pagan idols and ordered them destroyed, he did believe that the pagan sacred space could be re- deemed and transformed into a suitable place for sincere Christian worship. Seeing nothing inherently evil about the physical structures themselves and showing little concern that pagan memories of worship would overcome the English upon entering such buildings, Gregory still showed much sen- sitivity to the local people in giving this direction. He wanted them to feel comfortable worshipping as Christians in familiar surroundings. In short, Gregory was asserting a form of contextualization by redeeming sacred space rather than by destroying it and building new spaces.

Similarly, Gregory believed that pagan festivals could also be trans- formed into opportunities for Christian worship. Referring to a certain festival where cattle were sacrificed, he advised Augustine: "And because they are in the habit of slaughtering much cattle as sacrifices to devils, some solemnity ought to be given them in exchange for this . . . Do not let them sacrifice animals to the devil, but let them slaughter animals for their own food to the praise of God, and let them give thanks to the Giver of all things for His bountiful provision."[26] Again, with no tolerance for pagan idolatry, which he regarded as synonymous with worshipping the devil, Gregory as- serted that a festival like this could continue if the object of worship (the one true God) and the heart of worship (thanksgiving) became properly oriented.

In short, Gregory was urging Augustine and his team of monks to contextualize Christian worship in familiar English forms given their pagan past. While Gregory appears to show much sensitivity to and even appreciation for the host culture, he also seems to be a bit of a realist and acknowledged that the conversion of a people takes time and that mis- sionaries must be patient. He writes: "it is doubtless impossible to cut out everything at once from their stubborn minds. As when one climbs a high

25. Bede, *Ecclesiastical History* 1.30.
26. Ibid.

mountain, one does not advance in great strides, but slowly and surely by small steps."[27]

Jesus Mosques?

In reading Gregory's advice to Augustine on how redeeming sacred space that has previously been used for pagan worship, this raises some important questions for global church planting today. Many church planters in the West will resonate with Gregory's advice as they are establishing congregations that meet in movie theatres, bars, and public school facilities. There are many advantages to renting an already built structure at a reasonable price. Plus, a neutral location like a movie theatre or school surely appeals to many unchurched types who would not enter a "churchy" looking building.

But moving away from the western context, what if the facility is a mosque or a Buddhist temple? What if communities of Muslims in Asia or Africa embrace the gospel and the mosque is the best available structure to accommodate corporate worship? What if Buddhist leaders in Asia allowed new churches to use their temples for church services? Do the architecture and symbols of sacred space (e.g., Muslim, Buddhist, pagan) affect the worldview of a Christian worshipper? Is a former Muslim able to worship the God of the Bible in his former place of worship? Would other Muslims see this follower of Christ as a distinct follower of Christ if he continues to pray and worship in a mosque? In short, how does Bishop Gregory's advice apply to such contexts of mission today?

A second example of contextualization related to pagan sacred space is found in Boniface's eighth-century mission to Germany. As discussed, this missionary monk from England became known for "felling the sacred oak of Thor at Geismar in Hesse, the chief object of the superstitious reverence of the non-Christians and of the half-Christianized peoples of that area."[28] At first glance, it seems that Boniface's approach was not at all contextual and it was certainly far removed from Gregory's advice to Augustine in the English context. However, as these mission activities have been described as a "conflict not between men but between the gods," Boniface's actions did in fact connect with the German traditions of "trial by ordeal."[29] Neill explains: "The Germans were convinced that anyone who infringed the sacredness of the sanctuary would be destroyed by the gods; Boniface affirmed that he would be unscathed. The oak was felled; nothing happened. The watchers were at once convinced that Boniface was right,

27. Ibid.
28. Neill, *History of Christian Missions*, 64. 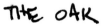 THE OAK
29. Ibid., 65.

and that the God he proclaimed was really stronger than the gods of their fathers."[30] Resembling Elijah's standoff with the prophets of Baal, Boniface's actions did seem to connect with the German appreciation for spiritual power encounters.[31] Though he enjoyed the military protection of Frankish King Charles Martel, it was the German perception that Boniface's god was more powerful than their deities that led to their conversion after their sacred space was destroyed.[32] Of course, as Wilken notes, the ongoing success of Boniface's ministry was in his follow-up: "cultivating good relations with local royalty and aristocracy, establishing new monasteries . . . copying books of the Scripture, baptizing, preaching and teaching."[33]

Both Gregory (via Augustine) and Boniface contextualized the gospel with regard to pagan sacred space. While the English seemed more attached to their places of worship, the Germans were apparently more intrigued by divine power. In both cases, the missionaries seemed to understand the worldview of their host people and, while both were deeply troubled by pagan idolatry, they addressed the issue of sacred space in a contextual manner.

Visual Culture

Though often overlooked by scholars, one fascinating means of understanding Christian history is through the study of visual and material culture. Robin Jensen, a visual culture specialist of the early Christian period, writes: "The term 'visual culture' encompasses images and artifacts produced by artists or artisans that reflect aspects of civilization which may or may not be evident in other cultural artifacts such as written documents."[34] Such artifacts, including lamps, mosaics, and architecture, offer a window into the daily life and worldview of early Christians. Discussing their value, especially in relation to written texts, Jensen adds: "Far more than mere illustration of the ideas or teachings articulated in surviving written documents, visual and material artifacts add depth and perspective to the analysis of a particular Christian group . . . one does not interpret the other, but both are understood as works of interpretation in their own terms. At the same

---

30. Ibid.

31. 1 Kgs 18:17–40.

32. Irvin and Sunquist, *History of the World Christian Movement*, 345–46

33. Wilken, *First Thousand Years*, 277.

34. Jensen, "Material Evidence (2): Visual Culture," 105.

time, they are not altogether independent and unrelated."[35] While visual culture can tell us about church history, I suggest that there is also much to be learned about the history of missions, including contextualization.

In addition to what has been briefly presented about the Nestorians' use of the lotus cross symbol in China, let us further support this claim by considering the mission of Columba and his monks in the late sixth century to the Pictish people of Scotland. According to Cummins, the Picts were "the first British nation to emerge from the tribal societies . . . from the fourth to the ninth century, they flourished and were the dominant power in the north [of Britain]."[36] Comprised of northern and southern clans, the Picts were first evangelized by Ninian in the late fourth and early fifth centuries. However, as discussed, the most fruitful mission work was accomplished by Columba and his monks beginning around 565 when the Irish abbot made favorable contact with the Pictish King Brute who embraced the gospel and gave the monks the island of Iona for their monastery, while allowing them the freedom to preach among the Picts.[37]

For years, art historians have been intrigued by the Pictish contribution to Insular Art, the predominant style of art in the British Isles from ca. 600–900. Though also known for their book art, the Picts were especially adept at metal work and stone art.[38] Employing many symbols and as many as fifty different animal figures, the Picts constructed grave stones as well as monuments to commemorate their history, including things like military victories.[39] Henderson and Henderson have grouped Pictish stone art into three periods or classes that also coincide with their spiritual history. They argue that the Class I artifacts belong to the "pre-conversion" or pre-Christian period because of their "pagan symbolism."[40] In the Class II period, the primary goal of Pictish stone art was to represent the cross, which the Hendersons regard as "a consequence of [their] conversion." In fact, they argue that in this period, the primary function of Insular sculpture in greater Britain was "to display the cross publicly."[41] Finally, Class III

35. Ibid., 104–6.

36. Cummins, *Age of the Picts*, 1.

37. Ibid., 82–89.

38. Henderson and Henderson, *Art of the Picts*, offers a helpful introduction and visual survey.

39. Ibid., 125–27, 134–35.

40. Henderson and Henderson, *Art of the Picts*, 10.

41. Ibid., 28.

stone art contained images of the cross that were completely free of pagan images.[42]

While the three periods of stone art show evidence that the Picts accepted Christianity and were apparently growing in their devotion to it, there is also evidence that Columba and his missionary band were deliberate in using this art form to communicate the gospel. The Hendersons argue that the cross-marked stone, "originated, without a doubt, in Irish missionary work among the Picts in the sixth and seventh centuries . . . the conformity in every respect with the cross-marked stones on Iona, and in the West of Scotland generally, is in itself evidence for the period at which Christianity began, literally, to make its mark on Pictland."[43] Simply put, Insular stone crosses communicated the essence of the gospel—the death, burial and resurrection of Christ. The Hendersons add: "when the first Irish or British missionaries introduced to the Picts the idea of carving a cross on a stone they will also have explained how the Christian symbol could function in a Christian society. It would primarily be as the embodiment of the central belief of the church that Christ's sufferings on the cross and his subsequent resurrection gave mankind the hope of eternal life. The cross was the basic aid for instruction and devotion."[44] In short, Columba and his monks used this key text of Pictish culture to not only communicate the essence of the gospel but also to offer the Pictish church a visual catechism as it instructed new believers.

While these initial stone crosses aided the monks in communicating the gospel through a medium familiar to the Picts, over time other crosses were constructed that communicated more of the overall story of Scripture. One example is St. Martin's cross, a large stone work built between 750 and 800 at Iona, which stands there in the present day. At the center of the cross, the birth of Christ is depicted with Mary holding the baby Jesus. Continuing down the cross, the stories of Daniel in the lions' den, Abraham raising his sword to sacrifice Isaac, David fighting Goliath, and David playing his

42. Ibid., 10.
43. Ibid., 159.
44. Ibid., 161.

Figure 7: St. Martin's cross at Iona.

harp are also communicated. The latter image seems especially contextual as David is joined by another musician playing triple pipes. In short, in viewing St. Martin's cross, Pictish visitors to Iona could contemplate the meaning of the cross and also engage in a visual Bible study.[45]

The gospel was further communicated through one of the most famous artifacts of Insular Art, the Book of Kells, which was developed at Iona around 800. Though it only included the four Latin Gospels, a mix of both Old and Vulgate Latin, the work was much longer because of its beautiful calligraphy and many pages of colorful illustrations, especially those relating New Testament stories.[46]

Let us consider how the Book of Kells was influenced by Pictish art and, in turn, how it became a significant means of clarifying the gospel for the Picts. First, though a book, the style of art in the Book of Kells greatly resembles the features of Pictish stone art. The many crosses displayed throughout the book look like the crosses on Iona and around Pictland. According to Meehan, their function was to offer the reader a regular reminder of the death, burial, and resurrection of Christ.[47] Second, the Book of Kells is rich in animal imagery, including snakes, birds, and lions, which also resemble the animals used in pre-Christian Pictish art. These are especially important for conveying the person and work of Christ. Though depicted as a human being at his birth, Christ is rendered as a calf in his death, as a snake shedding skin in the process of his resurrection, and as a lion in the resurrection. Also, he is presented as a peacock because of his perfect, authentic flesh and later as a fish because of having gone through the waters of baptism. The last image was probably particularly meaningful to those near the island of Iona where fishing was still a way of life.[48] The human depictions of Christ also seemed very contextual as he was rendered "blond, youthful, and radiant"; that is, he looked very Pictish and Irish in the pages of the Book of Kells.[49]

It should be remembered that the Book of Kells was forged in a liturgical and catechetical context. Though small and portable enough to be carried on mission trips around Pictland, the Book of Kells probably stayed

---

45. Tabraham, *Iona Abbey and Nunnery,* 9; also "Royal Commission on the Ancient and Historical Monuments of Scotland."

46. Meehan, *Book of Kells,* 78.

47. Ibid., 30–33.

48. Ibid., 41, 50–65

49. Ibid., 50.

at Iona for the most part. However, as there were many visitors who came to the island, including those who participated in the liturgical assemblies, the visual themes conveyed in the books (the person and work of Christ, the cross, as well as other Eucharistic imagery) served to instruct new believers.[50] In turn, these Bible stories and their truths traveled throughout the Scottish highlands in a manner that was meaningful and relevant to Pictish culture and their visual and oral memory. Obviously, one of the reasons that the Book of Kells was effective in this way was because of the excellent and beautiful work of art that it was. In 1185, Giraldus Cambrinsus commented to that end: "if you take the trouble to look closely, and penetrate to your eyes to the secrets of the artistry, you will notice such intricacies, so delicate and so subtle, so close together, and well-knitted, so involved and bound together, and so fresh still in their colorings that you will not hesitate to declare that all these things must have been the work, not of men, but of angels."[51]

In short, the influence of Pictish stone and book art is quite apparent when we study the symbols of Pictish Christianity, particularly artifacts such as St. Martin's cross and the Book of Kells. Further, because Columba and the generations of Ionan monks that followed embraced these art forms, it seems evident that they were being deliberately contextual in their mission strategy to convey the gospel through the building material of local Pictish culture.

50. Adomnan spoke of visitors to the island: *Life of Columba* 1.4, 25–27, 30, 32.
51. Cited in Meehan, *Book of Kells*, 89.

Figure 8: Book of Kells page showing Christ (source: Wikimedia Commons).

Work Culture

A final way that contextualization efforts were apparent in early Christian mission was through the lifestyles of Nestorian missionary merchants along the Silk Road. Describing this eastern marketplace context, Phillip Jenkins writes: "Throughout late antiquity and the Middle Ages, the legendary Silk Road ran from Syria into northern Persia and into what are now the nations of Uzbekistan and Turkmenistan. Beyond Merv, travelers crossed the Oxus River (the Amu Darya) to enter central Asia proper, and reached Bukhara and Samarkand. The route ultimately took them over forty-five hundred miles, into the heart of China."[52] Invigorating the Byzantine markets with

52. Jenkins, *Lost History of Christianity*, 52.

Chinese silk in the mid-sixth century, the Nestorians also seemed quite adept at connecting with other merchants in Central and East Asia.[53] This work, an authentic livelihood, became a platform that enabled these laborers—including monks and other merchants—to evangelize the eastern world. In fact, Jenkins points out that "Syriac Christian writers used the word merchant as a metaphor for those who spread the gospel."[54] He illustrates this further by citing a Syriac hymn that celebrated missionary merchants:

> Travel well girt like merchants,
> That we may gain the world.
> Convert men to me,
> Fill creation with teaching.[55]

How did the Nestorians contextualize the gospel? Though some arguments have been made earlier in the chapter for how the Nestorians articulated the gospel in a Chinese Buddhist context and while Nestorian church planting in the East has been well documented, in the current section, contextualizing the message has not been considered at all. Rather, what is significant to show in this brief discussion—and arguably the Nestorian's lasting legacy—is that they succeeded in contextualizing the messenger. Indeed, the message and the messenger ought to go hand in hand.

Marketplace Missionaries?

The Nestorians were distinct in history because of their ability to do business well in the Central Asian marketplace. As they worked with excellence, they also apparently had a robust verbal witness. In more recent Protestant missions history—especially since the eighteenth century and in the western world—being a missionary has been an identifiable vocation. Cross-cultural laborers, sustained financially through denominational funding or through the gifts of faith promise partners, have gone full-time to engage in evangelism, church planting, and gospel-focused development work. But is this the only missionary calling? What if a Christian trains as a teacher, engineer, or nurse and enters the marketplace—in his or her home country or abroad—and glorifies God through excellent work while also appropriately sharing a verbal witness? Should they not also be considered

---

53. Ibid., 64, 66.
54. Ibid., 63.
55. Ibid.

(*continued*)
missionaries? Shouldn't the leaders of the church call forward such ambassadors for Christ, lay hands on them, and send them out to labor in the harvest? In short, how does the Nestorian story challenge our paradigm for the missionary calling?

Conclusion

Before summarizing this chapter, we should also point out that there were many examples of failing to contextualize the gospel in early Christianity. In the western church, Latin language and culture remained dominant where it should not have been. As shown, this was the case in North Africa where the Scriptures were never translated into the Punic-Berber languages. While Latin was important for urban centers like Carthage or even Hippo, it was not sufficient for even nearby communities and villages. Though we celebrate the ministry of Patrick of Ireland and Augustine of Canterbury, including their contextualization strategies, it is somewhat surprising that the primary language of Scripture and worship in the British Isles remained Latin.[56] While the evangelization of Nubia (between northern Sudan and southern Egypt) ought to be regarded positively, the fact that the Nubian church adopted the Coptic Scriptures from neighboring Egypt was a missed opportunity for them to be a culturally Nubian church. Finally, one of the great shortcomings of the church in Christian history was the failure to plant a truly indigenous Arab church. Samuel Moffet writes: "It is worth noting that a significant weakness in the early Christian missions in Arabia was that the major areas of Christian strength were all foreign dominated . . . the Christian faith retained a foreign tinge in the Arabian Peninsula. Nowhere was it able to establish an authentic Arab base. It had not yet even translated the Scriptures in to Arabic."[57] As a result, there was really no biblically founded response to the rise of Islam in the early seventh century—a movement that quickly became a global religion.

Despite these shortcomings, this chapter has shown evidence of sincere efforts to contextualize the gospel. This was accomplished through early Christian missionaries being conversant with ideas and forms of communication, through redeeming sacred space and pre-existing festivals,

---

56. Thomas, *Christianity in Roman Britain*, 62–63.

57. Moffet, *History of Christianity in Asia*, 1:281.

through connecting with visual culture, and through understanding the marketplace. Through these approaches, the gospel began to take root among many people groups and regions testifying to the value that Christianity is a faith that ought to be at home in every culture, while also bringing transformation to that culture.

Questions for Reflection

1. Read 1 Corinthians 9:19–23:

> For though I am free from all, I have made myself a servant to all, that I might win more of them. To the Jews I became as a Jew, in order to win Jews. To those under the law I became as one under the law (though not being myself under the law) that I might win those under the law. To those outside the law I became as one outside the law (not being outside the law of God but under the law of Christ) that I might win those outside the law. To the weak I became weak, that I might win the weak. I have become all things to all people, that by all means I might save some. I do it all for the sake of the gospel, that I may share with them in its blessings.

   What contextualization strategies from the early church might benefit missions efforts today?

2. Some early Christian missionaries like Justin and Origen were clearly brilliant and well educated. Is it a worthwhile endeavor to do further studies (formally or informally) in order to engage with non-believing intellectuals?

3. Gregory encouraged Augustine to redeem pagan buildings and festivals for God's glory. How could we envision doing this today? What are the benefits and potential dangers of such an approach?

4. The monks from Iona clearly understood Pictish stone and book art and used these forms to communicate the gospel. How can the gospel be communicated through the arts today?

5. The Nestorians were contextualized messengers in the Central Asian marketplace. What does that look like today as believers witness unto Christ in the marketplace?

7

Word and Deed

"GOD HAS OPENED DOORS TO work with refugees and we have seen people healed and desiring to follow God."[1] These are the words of a Brazilian missionary describing the nature of his current ministry among refugees in the Arab world. With an evident commitment to proclaiming the person and work of Christ, such Brazilian laborers regard evangelism as central to their mission work. Yet, about half of the Brazilian mission community serving among Arabs indicated that humanitarian work was also a vital part of their ministry. Indeed, many are serving as doctors, nurses, and community health volunteers, while others care for the needs of women, the handicapped, and refugees. Brazilians, along with other Latin Americans, have also cultivated a theology in which evangelism and compassion ministries are intuitively integrated and there is an apparent conviction to minister to the whole person.[2]

While no one would question the conviction and courage of such missionaries, the relationship between proclamation and social action, especially when it comes to defining Christian mission, has not been without controversy and has been particularly debated among North American missiologists.[3] What is the relationship between ministry in Word (procla-

1. Smither, *Brazilian Evangelical Missions in the Arab World*, 173.

2. Ibid., 211–30.

3. For recent discussion on holistic mission and prioritism, see Hesslegrave, *Paradigms in Conflict*, 119–39; Little, "What Makes Mission Christian?"; McQuilkin et al., "Response"; and Russell, "Christian Mission is Holistic."

mation) and deed (caring for human needs)? Is proclamation alone insufficient, especially when missionaries serve among the poor and destitute? Is the integrity of the gospel compromised when the church does good deeds but does not tell the good news? While such questions ought to be resolved through continual reading of Scripture and appropriate theologizing, perhaps the long view of missions history might also be of assistance. In the current chapter, we will explore evidence for ministries of good works that accompanied proclamation in early Christian mission. Such deed ministry will include care for the poor, hungry, imprisoned, enslaved, and marginalized; but also ministry to those in need of healing and freedom from demonic oppression.

Caring for the Poor and Disenfranchised

During his short reign from 361 to 363, the Emperor Julian (known as the "apostate") penned these famous words in a letter to Arsacius, the pagan high priest of Galatia: "The impious Galileans (Christians) support not only of their own poor but ours as well."[4] This off-handed remark from an anti-Christian emperor actually supports the general description of how the early church engaged those on the margins of society—the poor, orphans, widows, the sick, prisoners, and slaves.[5] However, more than simply caring for the disenfranchised within local communities, such ministry also figured into the church's mission across cultures. Irvin and Sunquist helpfully assert: "Through their social relief activities, Christians had gained a reputation that reached beyond their immediate numbers. Churches cared for the sick and dying during the period that plagues swept through the urban regions, for instance. They raised funds to ransom prisoners and slaves, gathered food to provide for the hungry, and assisted sailors who had been shipwrecked. Such efforts did much to boost the Christian ranks, as much as the other evangelistic activities that churches undertook."[6]

Discussing the relationship between evangelism and caring for human needs, Blocher and Blandenier argue, "The oral proclamation of the gospel [was] not disincarnated; it [was] accompanied by acts of charity,

---

4. Cited in Hinson, *Church Triumphant*, 162; also Wilken, *First Thousand Years*, 158.

5. Cf. Harnack, *Mission and Expansion of Christianity*, 149; Bosch, *Transforming Mission*, 49.

6. Irvin and Sunquist, *History of the World Christian Movement*, 99.

service and the *diakonia* ("care" or "service") of Christians."[7] While Blocher and Blandenier are describing first-century mission, their remarks actually characterize mission throughout the period of our study. Let us support this claim by examining the work of missionary monks and then by focusing on the ministries of some church leaders.

Monastic Missions

As shown, the most significant movement of laborers involved in intercultural mission from the fifth century on were missionary monks.[8] Monastic theology and practice were largely built on two principles—prayer (*ora*) and labor (*labora*).[9] Indeed, many of the duties performed by monks, such as gardening or weaving mats, were done to deliberately help the monk focus on prayer. As monastic thought on work developed, these acts of labor—farming, copying books, and even preaching—came to be regarded as acts of worship in their own right.[10] Reflecting theologically on the nature of work, the fourth-century monk Evagrius of Pontus believed that work was a means for the monk to make spiritual progress while providing for his needs and the needs of others; but he was also persuaded that work should be done with excellence and integrity. For Evagrius, monastic labor was a veritable form of worship.[11]

At points in the history of monasticism, there was disagreement over the relationship and balance between the contemplative (*ora*) and active (*labora*) elements of monastic living. Wilken notes that Basil of Caesarea, whom we will discuss shortly, "became critical of self-absorbed hermits." Basil believed that "the solitary life of prayer would be complemented by the active life. Contemplation and service were to go hand in hand."[12] Indeed, such monastic activism manifested itself in part through mission work characterized by preaching and service. For example, the missionary monks in northern Europe seemed to have an impact on the local populations because of their holy lifestyles, exemplary service, and hard work. Noll helpfully writes: "The missionary effectiveness of the monks usually

7. Blocher and Blandenier, *Evangelization of the World,* 11.
8. Cf. Wilken, *First Thousand Years,* 108.
9. Ibid., 107; also Noll, *Turning Points,* 86–91.
10. Bosch, *Transforming Mission,* 235.
11. Smither, "Lessons from a Tentmaking Ascetic," 490–93.
12. Wilken, *First Thousand Years,* 105.

depended as much upon their plain virtues as upon more highly visible exertions in preaching or teaching. For a monastery to be established in a pagan area allowed the local population to see the application of Christianity to daily existence, as monks tilled the soil, welcomed visitors, and carried out the offices of study and daily prayer. So arose the saying that monks civilized Europe *cruce, libro, et atro*—with cross, book, and plow."[13]

Emerging in the sixth century, the Benedictines are also remembered for their participation in Europe's agricultural revolution as part of their mission. Describing this, Guizot writes that they "were the agriculturalists of Europe; they cleared it on a large scale associating agriculture with preaching."[14] Newman adds rather poetically, "They found a swamp, a moor, a thicket, a rock, and they made an Eden in the wilderness."[15]

Around the same time in France, the Irish monk Columban founded a monastery at Luxeuil that became a missionary training center for monks committed to ministry in Word and deed. Describing the approach to learning and the monastery's overall ethos, Blocher and Blandenier write that "theology as well as classical and ancient letters, and agriculture were taught there. The sick were also cared for."[16]

In the East, the Nestorian missions movement also showed signs of Word and deed ministry. Moffet notes that in the fifth century, the Nestorians included literacy training in their mission approach: "It was through Arab Christians of Hirta [modern Iraq] that desert Arabs were taught Syriac and learned to read and write."[17] As the Nestorians continued their ministry between Persia and China, they also established monasteries that, according to Irvin and Sunquist, served as "centers of worship and evangelism, but also inns for Christian merchants, centers of medical care, and even schools."[18] Some of the missionary monks that came from Syria were also trained as doctors and they put that training to use in evangelizing Central Asia.[19]

13. Noll, *Turning Points*, 92.

14. Cited in Newman, *Rise and Progress*, 399.

15. Ibid, 398.

16. Blocher and Blandenier, *Evangelization of the World*, 66; cf. Bosch, *Transforming Mission*, 232.

17. Moffet, *History of Christianity in Asia*, 1:276–77.

18. Irvin and Sunquist, *History of the World Christian Movement*, 305.

19. Ibid., 312.

Church Leaders

In addition to the missionary monastic movements, bishops and other church leaders also shared a conviction for Word and deed ministry. Wilken' writes: "Over time, caring for the poor and needy came to be seen as a primary responsibility of the <u>bishop</u>. In a mid-third-century letter to the bishop of Antioch, the bishop of Rome casually remarked that his church supported fifteen hundred widows and persons in need. In . . . North Africa, the church had in its storehouse shirts for men and veils for women, dresses and shoes for women, as well as containers of oil and wine for the hungry."[20] Let us examine these values in the ministries of leaders who were also ministering across cultures.

One such example is Ephraem the Syrian, the most famous theologian of the fourth-century Syriac church who is best remembered for articulating theology in the form of hymns and poetry. Originally from Persia, Ephraem spent the last decade of his life caring for the poor in Edessa, especially those who were afflicted by famine and the plague. Ephraem's service included organizing a food drive for the hungry and founding a hospital in Edessa. Citing in part the church historian Sozomen, Holman describes Ephraem's ministry: "In the late 360s, Ephraem became the steward of funds to provide for victims of famine in Edessa. As soon as the rich gave him their supply, he 'had about three hundred beds fitted up in the public porches and here he tended those that were ill and suffering from the effects of the famine.'"[21] Sozomen's observation that Ephraem's ministry audience included "foreigners or natives of the surrounding country" certainly highlights the intercultural and non-discriminatory nature of his work. Finally, Ephraem apparently shared the gift of his theologically rich hymns with the afflicted as these songs proved to be a comfort to those who were sick and dying. In the midst of such courageous service, Ephraem died in 373.[22]

During this same period, because of the great needs of the hungry, poor, and oppressed, a number of church leaders made the radical decision to sell the precious metals that adorned the altars and that were used for sacramental vessels during worship assemblies. In the fourth century in Constantinople, a deacon named Marathonius liquidated the church's sacred ornaments to purchase food for victims of famine. In the fifth century,

20. Wilken, *First Thousand Years*, 157.

21. Sozomen, *History of the Church*, 3:16, cited in Holman, *Hungry Are Dying*, 60.

22. Irvin and Sunquist, *History of the World Christian Movement*, 198.

Acacius of Amida (Mesopotamia) acted similarly and got involved with a humanitarian crisis resulting from military campaigns in the eastern part of the Roman Empire. Holman notes that Acacius "convinced his clergy to sell the altar vessels to redeem seven thousand Persian prisoners who had been taken by the Romans in their attack on Azazene. The prisoners were dying of starvation. Acacius not only ransomed the prisoners but also then fed them . . . and eventually sent them back to Persia."[23] In the fourth and fifth centuries, Ambrose of Milan (ca. 340–397) in the West and Rabula of Edessa also liquidated the church's material wealth to ransom prisoners and meet the needs of the poor.[24]

The Gospel in Word and *Futbol*

In a highly restricted region in the Middle East, two Brazilian soccer (futbol) coaches have been able to connect with a displaced people group through their sport. With the blessing of community leaders, the coaches organized a soccer school for the children who have little to occupy themselves with on a daily basis and little to hope for in the future. Though they are not free to evangelize openly, the coaches convey life skills based on biblical principles in their coaching curriculum. Hence, "with a soccer ball and jersey, they have accessed places where [western] doctors and teachers have never been allowed to enter" and minister in this otherwise tense area.[25] Some organizations such as the Brazilian Baptist Convention have developed a similar soccer and evangelism strategy and are training many of their personnel around the world to implement it. However, for many Brazilian missionaries, soccer remains simply a natural way to exercise, build relationships, and share the gospel. One worker related: "I love using sports—something I really enjoy—for ministry."[26]

Basil of Caesarea

While these church leaders showed exemplary care for the needy, the ministry of the fourth-century bishop Basil of Caesarea merits additional discussion.[27] Having been raised in an ascetic family, Basil, after studies in philosophy and rhetoric, pursued his own monastic withdrawal. This

23. Ibid.

24. Ibid.

25. Smither, *Brazilian Evangelical Missions in the Arab World*, 177.

26. Ibid., 178.

27. Some of the thoughts in this section are adapted from my article, "Basil of Caesarea: An Early Christian Model of Urban Ministry."

included pursuing a monastic mentor, Eustathius of Sebaste, and then later establishing a community at his family's estate in Pontus where he was joined by Gregory of Nazianzus (329–ca.390). During his time with Eustathius, Basil apparently developed some deeper convictions about ministry to the poor. Due to the Arian controversy that continued to fester in Asia Minor, Basil felt compelled to accept ordination in the church at Caesarea, eventually becoming its bishop in 370. Despite accepting this ecclesiastical calling, Basil continued to pursue a monastic way of life, placing him among a growing group of fourth- and fifth-century monk-bishops that included the likes of Eusebius of Vercellae (283–371), Martin of Tours, Gregory of Nazianzus, John Chrysostom (347–407), and Augustine of Hippo. To be sure, Basil's monastic theology influenced his thoughts on the bishop's obligation to the poor and needy.[28]

Basil's ministry context was Caesarea, which had been the capital of the Roman province of Cappadocia since the early first century following a declaration by the Emperor Claudius. Economically speaking, Caesarea was not very prosperous and its agricultural industry generally struggled. Conditions only worsened in the third century when earthquakes destroyed parts of Pontus and Cappadocia.[29] Despite these difficulties, Caesarea was an important city because of some key Roman roads—trade routes that stretched from Constantinople to Syria—that ran through the city. On one hand, this was beneficial to Caesarea because travelling merchants would stop in the city, lodge there, and spend money in its establishments. On the other hand, the roads also brought the Roman army, including some troops that commandeered local food sources and other supplies creating stress for the local inhabitants. Understanding Caesarea's strategic geographic location, the Roman government established the city as one of its key administrative centers. Finally, the city's location also made it an important intercultural crossroads as diverse peoples from Asia Minor, Armenia, Syria, Persia, and the northern Gothic regions regularly spent time and interacted in Caesarea.[30]

28. Rousseau, *Basil of Caesarea*, 4–5, 25–27, 68–69, 84–85, 93; Sterk, *Renouncing the World Yet Leading the Church*, 39–40, 43–46, 73–76.

29. McHugh, "Cappadocia," 213.

30. Rousseau, *Basil of Caesarea*, 133–34; Holman, *Hungry are Dying*, 69–70; Wilken, *First Thousand Years*, 154.

Figure 9: Basilica of Peace at Hippo where Augustine preached.

There were a number of challenges that Basil faced as he led the church in Caesarea. First, though the region had been evangelized largely in the third century by Gregory Thaumaturgus, Basil battled against Arian theology that was prominent among the clergy of Asia Minor and also adhered to by some so-called Christian emperors. In fact, the Emperor Valens divided Cappadocia in half in an apparent deliberate effort to limit Basil's influence because of Basil's Nicene convictions.[31]

Another significant challenge that Basil faced was poverty. In an insightful study on poverty in the early church period, Holman suggests that there were two categories of poverty, *penes and ptochos*. She writes: "*Ptochos* traditionally designated the destitute beggar who is outside or at the fringes of society, the 'street person,' the extreme poor. *Penes*, on the other hand, is used to indicate the individual whose economic resources were minimal but who functioned within society, the 'working poor.'"[32] Basil speaks a bit more directly to the causes of these types of poverty by asserting, "I consider that a *ptochos* is he who falls from wealth into need; but a *penes*

31. Smither, "Basil of Caesarea," 80–81.

32. Holman, *Hungry Are Dying*, 5.

is he who is in need from the first and is acceptable to the Lord."[33] While both poverty-stricken groups could be found in Caesarea, Basil's sermons suggest that the *ptochoi* represented the most common type of poverty. In some cases, this included desperate families abandoning children on the doorstep of the church at Caesarea.[34]

The biggest factor that contributed to Caesareans slipping into poverty was the famine that hit Cappadocia in 368. It is impossible to understand Basil's ministry without having a sense of this period of tragedy. Gregory of Nazianzus described it in these words: "There was a famine, the most severe one ever recorded. The city was in distress and there was no source of assistance . . . The hardest part of all such distress is the insensibility and insatiability of those who possess supplies . . . Such are the buyers and sellers of corn."[35] Holman adds that there had been "an extremely cold, dry winter that had been followed by an unusually hot, dry spring, and this led to catastrophic agricultural crisis as wells and rivers dried up and crops failed. Those able to hoard grain increased their vigilance and the market prices. Laborers began to starve. Schools closed down. The populace came to church to pray for rain. The poor who worked in the fields and wandered along the roads took on the appearance of living cadavers. Possibly the poor resorted to exposing their children, or selling them, while the rich haggled with them over the purchase price."[36] Based on evidence from Basil's letters, the famine probably lasted for four years and it led to other social and health problems. For example, in 372, there was a riot in Caesarea. As noted, some responded by hoarding grain, while others resorted to stealing. From Basil's sermons, we are also given a picture of the slow and horrible death that some were dying from starvation.[37]

How did Basil respond to the poverty related issues that developed in Caesarea? First, his preaching was characterized by a prophetic discourse in which he called the Caesareans to pursue righteousness regardless of their situation.[38] He rebuked the money lenders for exploiting the poor by charging exorbitant interest rates. On the other hand, Basil chastised the poor themselves for borrowing the money instead of being content in their

---

33. Basil, *Short Rules* 262, cited in Holman, *Hungry are Dying,* 6.

34. Ibid., 78–80.

35. Gregory of Nazianzus, *Oration* 43.34 cited in Holman, *Hungry are Dying,* 65

36. Ibid., 68–69.

37. Basil, *Letters* 31, 86; Holman, "The Hungry Body," 339.

38. Ibid., 338.

circumstances and patient with the process of economic recovery. Basil also preached against those who hoarded grain during the famine as well as the wealthy who turned a blind eye to the poor and failed to be generous. Finally, as slavery only increased amid this turmoil, Basil preached prophetically against this social sin.[39]

Second, Basil used his position as bishop of Caesarea to be an advocate for the poor. Through writing letters and personal meetings, Basil successfully lobbied for tax relief for the poor and secured donations for some of his projects. Though as noted, Basil experienced much conflict with Valens, the bishop was able to convince the emperor to also contribute financially to the needs of the poor in Caesarea.[40]

Andrew Dinan observes that "Basil's solicitude for the welfare of his people was manifest in concrete ways,"[41] the first of which was actively responding to hunger. In an extended description, Gregory of Nazianzus describes Basil's courageous leadership and generosity in response to the famine of 368:

> By his word and advice [Basil] opened the stores of those who possessed them, and so, according to the Scripture, dealt food to the hungry and satisfied the poor with bread . . . and in what way? . . . He gathered together the victims of the famine with some who were but slightly recovering from it, men and women, infants, old men . . . and obtaining contributions of all sorts of food which can relieve famine, set before them basins of soup and such meat as was found preserved among us, on which the poor live. Then, imitating the ministry of Christ . . . he attended to the bodies and souls of those who needed it, combining personal respect with the supply of their necessity, and so giving them a double relief. Such was our young furnisher of corn, and second Joseph . . . [But unlike Joseph, Basil's] services were gratuitous and his succor of the famine gained no profit, having only one object, to win kindly feelings by kindly treatment, and to gain by his rations of corn the heavenly blessings.[42]

According to Gregory, Basil liquidated some of his own inherited assets to help meet the needs of the Caesareans: "[Basil] ungrudgingly spent upon the poor his patrimony even before he was a priest, and most of all in

LIQUIDATED RESOURCES AND GAVE TO POOR

---

39. Cf. Smither, "Basil of Caesarea," 83 86.

40. Ibid., 86–87; Wilken, *First Thousand Years*, 160.

41. Dinan, "Manual Labor in the Life and Thought of St. Basil," 135.

42. Gregory of Nazianzus, *Oration* 43.34–36, cited in Holman, *Hungry Are Dying*, 65.

the time of the famine, during which he was a ruler of the church, though still a priest in the rank of presbyters; and afterwards did not hoard even what remained to him."[43] Though Basil's brother Gregory of Nyssa likened him to Elijah, Gregory of Nazianzus described him as a Joseph for the people of Caesarea, a comparison with which Basil seemed to agree. In *Sermon 6*, Basil interpreted and applied the Joseph narratives from Genesis toward his ministry in Caesarea by proclaiming: "I shall open my barns. I shall be like Joseph in proclaiming the love of my fellow man."[44]

A second concrete expression of Basil's ministry to the poor was the establishment of the *basileas* ("new city")—"a complex of buildings constructed at the edge of Caesarea during the early years of Basil's episcopate."[45] Built on land owned by Basil's family or perhaps donated by the emperor, the complex was first called the *basileas* by the fifth-century church historian Sozomen who recorded: "the *basileas*, the most celebrated hospice for the poor. It was established by Basil, bishop of Caesarea, from whom it received its name in the beginning, and retains it until today."[46] While Basil was influenced by others to act on behalf of the poor, including his family and Eustathius, it seems that the devastation caused by the famine of 368 drove him to launch the *basileas* project.[47]

What were the specific ministries of the *basileas*? First, the complex included a home for the poor. Some of the residents probably included children that had been abandoned by their parents during the famine.[48] Second, the facility had a hospital that cared for the sick. Sterk suggests that some patients were probably suffering from leprosy.[49] Third, the *basileas* offered the poor an opportunity to work and to develop job skills.[50] Fourth, as noted, the complex included storehouses with food supplies administered by the "Joseph" of Caesarea.[51] Finally, as Caesarea was located on a

---

43. Gregory of Nazianzus, *Against Eunomius* 1.10, cited in Holman, *Hungry Are Dying*, 66

44. Basil, *Sermon* 6.2, cited in Holman, *Hungry Are Dying*, 128.

45. Sterk, *Renouncing the World Yet Leading the Church*, 69; cf. Wilken, *First Thousand Years*, 159–62.

46. Sozomen, *Ecclesiastical History* 6.34.9

47. Basil, *Letters* 94, 150, 176; Sterk, *Renouncing the World Yet Leading the Church*, 40, 69; Holman, *Hungry Are Dying*, 76.

48. Gregory of Nazianzus, *Oration* 43.35; Holman, *Hungry Are Dying*, 80.

49. Sterk, *Renouncing the World Yet Leading the Church*, 69.

50. Patitsas, "St. Basil's Philanthropic Program," 269; Holman, *Hungry Are Dying*, 74.

51. Rousseau, *Basil of Caesarea*, 142.

crossroads between Asia Minor, Syria, Armenia and the Gothic regions, the *basileas* included a hospitality house for travelers.[52] Basil insisted that his disciples be able to show hospitality to minister to other believers but also as a means to witness to non-Christians. In his *Long Rules,* he writes:

> Has a guest arrived? If he is a brother . . . he will recognize the fare we provide as properly his own. What he has left at home, he will find with us. Suppose he is weary after his journey. We then provide as much nourishment as is required to relieve his weariness. Is it a secular person who has arrived? Let him learn through actual experience . . . and let him be given a model and pattern of frugal sufficiency in matters of food . . . In every case, care must be taken for a good table, yet without overstepping the limits of the actual need. This should be our aim in hospitality—that the individual requirements of our guests may be cared for.[53]

For Basil, the *basileas* ministry was perhaps the clearest expression of what it meant for him to be a monk-bishop ministering in the city. Sterk writes: "for Basil, then, involvement in such a foundation was what committed ascetics as well as bishops ought to be doing. Such activity on the part of monks, bishops, and laity alike made the gospel a living reality in the city."[54] Basil's expectation was that the monastic community would be a community that served others. Distinguishing his communal monastic vision from those who withdrew into isolation, he simply asked: "Whose feet will you wash? For whom will you care? In comparison with whom will you be the least?"[55] Dinan adds that the goal of Basil's manual labor was charity—loving God and loving one's neighbor.[56] Further, Basil was convinced that an important task of a bishop or Christian leader was caring for the poor. He instructed spiritual leaders in his *Morals* that "the preacher of the Word should be compassionate and merciful, especially toward those who are suffering distress of soul" and be "solicitous even with regard to the bodily needs of those in our charge."[57] While clergy in Caesarea were involved in administrating the work of the *basileas,* Basil also encouraged other church leaders in Cappadocia and Asia Minor to make ministry to the

---

52. Ibid., 133.

53. Basil, *Long Rules* 20 (FC 5).

54. Sterk, *Renouncing the World Yet Leading the Church,* 71.

55. Basil, *Long Rules* 7, cited in Ramsey, *Beginning to Read the Church Fathers,* 180

56. Dinan, "Manual Labor in the Life and Thought of St. Basil," 147–49.

57. Basil, *Morals* 70.19–20.

poor a priority in their churches.[58] Indeed, there is evidence that a number
of smaller projects for the poor developed in Cappadocia under the leadership of bishops that Basil supervised.[59] In short, Basil's efforts appeared to
be sustainable as the *basileas* facility remained intact and ministry to the
poor continued for over a century after his death.[60]

As we conclude this discussion on Basil's ministry to the poor, the
question should be posed, how did Basil view the relationship between
proclamation and caring for human needs? While Basil's concern for the
poor and sick has been discussed, it should be noted that he regarded evangelism and preaching as central to his ministry. In his work *On the Holy
Spirit*, he praised the ministry of Gregory Thaumaturgus, the bishop who
helped transform Cappadocia in the third century through his evangelistic
preaching.[61] While Basil's preaching was intended to nourish the faithful,
he also preached in order to evangelize non-Christians as well.[62] In his
oration commemorating Basil's life, Gregory of Nazianzus seems to provide
the strongest evidence that Basil believed that the spiritual needs of the
Cappadocians were greater than their physical ones. He writes:

> [Basil] provided the nourishment of the Word and that more per-
> fect good work and distribution being from heaven and on high;
> if the bread of angels is the Word, whereby souls hungry for God
> are fed and given to drink, and seek after nourishment that neither
> diminishes nor fails but remains forever; thus [i.e., by his sermons]
> this supplier of grain and abundant riches [he who was] the poor-
> est and most needy [person] I have known, provided, not for a
> famine of bread or a thirst for water, but a longing for the truly
> life-giving and nourishing Word, which effects growth to spiritual
> maturity in those nourished well on it.[63]

In short, while Basil ministered in Word and in deed, he seems to have
taken more seriously the spiritual needs of his ministry audience.

58. Basil, *Letters* 142–43; Sterk, *Renouncing the World Yet Leading the Church*, 74;
Patitsas, "St. Basil's Philanthropic Program," 269, 282; Rousseau, *Basil of Caesarea*, 143.

59. Basil, *Letters* 141–44, 223; Rousseau, *Basil of Caesarea*, 149; Sterk, *Renouncing the
World Yet Leading the Church*, 69–70.

60. Holman, *Hungry Are Dying*, 75.

61. Basil, *On the Holy Spirit* 29.34; Sterk, *Renouncing the World Yet Leading the
Church*, 37

62. Basil, *Morals* 70.9–11, 31–34.

63. Gregory of Nazianzus *Oration* 43.36, cited in Holman, *Hungry Are Dying*, 65.

Miracles and Power Encounters

Ministry in Word and deed, as discussed in the previous pages, is most often understood as preaching the gospel and ministering to human needs, such as poverty and hunger. However, I would like to assert that early Christian deed ministry also included miracles, particularly in the way of healing, and spiritual power encounters. By power encounters, I am referring to instances in which missionaries confronted and cast out demons or evil spirits in Jesus' name. Though it may be reasonably argued that miracles and power encounters are merely ways of ministering to spiritual needs, I am choosing to regard it as more in the realm of deed because it involved more than proclaiming the gospel and often included intercession, exorcism, and confronting evil spirits.

I realize that modern scholars, including many evangelical Christians, are naturally skeptical toward the notion of healing and power encounters and such a discussion might be quickly dismissed. At this point, we who have grown up in the West in the post-Enlightenment period ought to recognize our worldview presuppositions, particularly the prevailing view that the world is best explained through reason and science—that there is a logical or empirical explanation for everything. But what we should equally recognize is that the pre-modern worldviews of patristic theologians like Justin, Irenaeus, Basil, Athanasius and, Augustine among others were not at all vexed by accounts of miracles or power encounters. In fact, each of these church fathers wrote about these things as accepted realities.[64] The repeated accounts of miracles and power encounters in patristic literature should in the very least move us to try to understand the early church's view toward the miraculous and spiritual world. Further, the aim of this section is to explore how such perspectives also informed early Christian mission.

Generally describing mission in the early church, Irvin and Sunquist observe, "Among the most prominent features in early Christian narratives are stories of miracles performed by the followers of Jesus in his name. We can assume that the impact of such signs and wonders was a significant factor."[65] In his *Second Apology,* addressed to the Roman Senate, Justin made these claims about power encounters: "There are throughout the world and in your city [Rome] a number of demon-possessed that neither

---

64. Smither, "To Emulate and the Imitate," 148.

65. Irvin and Sunquist, *History of the World Christian Movement*, 47; cf. Hvalvik, "In Word and Deed," 283–84.

pleas, nor enchantments, nor filters have been able to heal. Our Christians, abjuring them in the name of Jesus crucified under Pontius Pilate, have healed them of it and continue to heal many today."[66] Writing a few decades later, Irenaeus made a similar argument: "The true disciples of Christ have received a grace, they perform miracles in his name . . . Some really expel demons and, frequently, those they have freed from these evil spirits believe in Christ and join the church."[67]   GOSPEL + MIRACLES

Though skeptical about miracle stories, Ramsay MacMullen concedes that gospel proclamation and miracles were the most prominent reasons why pagans converted to Christianity in the Roman Empire both before and after the rise of Constantine.[68] MacMullen and Kreider also show that the church's understanding of the spiritual world influenced baptismal and catechetical practices, especially in the first five centuries.[69] As catechumens were instructed prior to baptism, they were prayed for and invited to renounce the influence of the Evil One. In the African context in particular, as new believers were baptized, they publicly declared that Jesus Christ was Lord while renouncing the works of Satan in their flesh. Finally, in the church at Milan in the fourth century, Ambrose's ministerial staff included exorcists who were available to intercede for those experiencing spiritual conflicts with demons.

The church's views on the spiritual world and the plausibility of miracles were not isolated to the early Christian centuries. Commenting on the church in the seventh century onward, Philip Jenkins makes the interesting assertion that Christianity was actually distinct from Islam because of its miraculous accounts. He writes, "All forms of Christianity, East or West, emphasized charismatic and miraculous themes, to a degree that separated them from more rationalistic Muslim contemporaries."[70]

66. Justin, *Second Apology* 6, cited in Blocher and Blandenier, *Evangelization of the World,* 35.

67. Irenaeus, *Against All Heresies* 2.23, cited in Blocher and Blandenier, *Evangelization of the World,* 35.

68. MacMullen, *Christianity and Paganism,* 30, 136–37.

69. MacMullen, *Christianizing the Roman Empire,* 27; Kreider, *Change of Conversion,* 16–17.

70. Jenkins, *Lost History of Christianity,* 75–76.

The Flaw of the Excluded Middle

In 1982, anthropologist Paul Hiebert published a ground-breaking article entitled, "The Flaw of the Excluded Middle." Reflecting largely on his experience ministering in India, where many struggled with sickness and disease, Hiebert concluded that there were three levels from which people looked at the world: a present worldview perceived by the senses; a cosmic, heavenly level focused on the afterlife; but also a middle level where spirits, ghosts, and other animate life forms inhabit the present world. Commenting on his journey in mission, Hiebert writes: "I had excluded the middle level of supernatural but this-worldly beings and forces from my own world view. As a scientist I had been trained to deal with the empirical world in naturalistic terms. As a theologian, I was taught to answer ultimate questions in theistic terms. For me the middle zone did not really exist. Unlike Indian villagers, I had given little thought to spirits of this world, to local ancestors and ghosts, or to the souls of animals … Consequently I had no answers to the questions they raised."[71]

Discussing the historic development of western thought and its implications for looking at the spiritual world, Hiebert adds: "The result was the secularization of science and the mystification of religion. Science dealt with the empirical world using mechanistic analogies, leaving religion to handle other-worldly matters, often in terms of organic analogies. Science was based on the certitudes of sense experience, experimentation and proof. Religion was left with faith in visions, dreams and inner feelings. Science sought order in natural laws. Religion was brought in to deal with miracles and exceptions to the natural order, but these decreased as scientific knowledge expanded."[72]

Explaining the resulting challenges for post-seventeenth century western missionaries going into many places in the world, he adds: "It should be apparent why many missionaries trained in the West had no answers to the problems of the middle level—they often did not even see it. When tribal people spoke of fear of evil spirits, they denied the existence of the spirits rather than claim the power of Christ over them."[73]

With a handle on the worldview of western missionaries and those of their host cultures, Hiebert proposes a way forward and suggests that missionaries should "develop holistic theologies that deal with all areas of life … On the highest level this includes a theology of God in cosmic history: in the creation, redemption, purpose and destiny of all things … On the middle level, a holistic theology includes a theology of God in human history: in the affairs of nations, of peoples and of individuals. This must include a theology of divine guidance, provision and healing; of ancestors, spirits and invisible powers of this world; and of suffering,

71. Hiebert, "Flaw of the Excluded Middle," 43.
72. Ibid.,
73. Ibid., 44.

(continued)
misfortune and death."[74] While Hiebert has offered valuable counsel to modern missionaries from the West, it seems also that much can be gleaned from how early Christian missionaries perceived the spiritual world and ministered because of it.

Having established the church's general regard for miracles and the spiritual world, let us consider some representative examples of how miracles and power encounters related to mission in this period. As noted, the ministry strategy of Gregory Thaumaturgus in third-century Asia Minor was quite diverse. In the process of preaching from Scripture, he connected with the educated and made the gospel clear in part through his command of philosophy, mathematics, and law. Further, his ministry also included power encounters and miracles. In his famous work, *On the Holy Spirit,* Basil described some of Gregory's daily ministry, which Basil regarded as carried out by the Spirit's power:

> From daybreak, a crowd of people were pressing at the door of Gregory—the old, those demon possessed, those unhappy in all respects—to whom he was in turn preaching, questioning, exhorting, healing. It was his manner to bring the people the gospel: the people were seeing the power of God as long as they were hearing him speak. Gregory had by the assistance of the Holy Spirit a redoubtable power over demons . . . it would take a long time to relate in detail the miracles of this man, who by reason of the superabundance of gifts (chrisms) that the Spirit was producing in him, such as works of power and signs and prodigies, was proclaimed a "second Moses" even by the enemies of the church.[75]

From this account, it seems that Gregory did not merely engage in exorcism or healing as an end to themselves; rather, these were tasks that accompanied the work of proclamation. Basil's further claim is that as pagans acknowledged the power of the Christian God, they believed Gregory's message.

As shown, in fourth-century Gaul, Martin of Tours served as a missionary-monk-bishop and labored to evangelize the pagan populations

---

74. Ibid., 45–46.

75. Basil, *On the Holy Spirit* 29 cited in Blocher and Blandenier, *Evangelization of the World,* 19.

through confronting pagan practices, destroying pagan temples, demonstrating a holy life, and performing healings and other miracles. Though acknowledging his practice at times of destroying temples, Irvin and Sunquist argue: "The most effective evangelistic practices . . . were in his miracles. In them, we catch a glimpse of the positive reasons why common people turned to the Christian God about whom Martin spoke. This holy man often saw visions, and he exorcised evil spirits from people who were possessed. Among the numerous miracles he is reported to have worked, many involved healing."[76] Sulpitius Severus' sacred biography of Martin records numerous miracles and power encounters; however, let us consider one example. He writes: "While Martin was in the process of knocking down a temple, a crowd of pagan peasants rushed upon him. One of them, more audacious than the others, having unsheathed a sword was going to strike him . . . [Martin] presented his neck to the assailant. The pagan did not hesitate to strike a blow, but in lifting his right arm too high, he fell over backwards. Struck immediately by a holy terror, he implored forgiveness." Severus continues, "[Martin] appeased the spirit of these pagans by the holiness of his preaching, enlightening them with the light of truth so that it was by their own hands that they demolished their temples."[77] Not unlike Gregory's ministry, Martin's power encounter was followed by a truth encounter in which he preached the gospel.

Some final examples of miracles and power encounters can be also observed in Columba's ministry among the Picts. In one account, Adomnan tells of a certain well that was inhabited by a demonic presence. Despite the fact that those who touched or drank the water became sick with leprosy, blindness, or other ailments, the well became a center for pagan devotion. Adomnan writes: "When St. Columba learned of this, he made his way fearlessly to the well. The wizards, whom he had often driven away in confusion and defeat, saw what he was doing and were glad, for they expected that he too should suffer the effects of touching the harmful water. The saint first raised his hands and called on the name of Christ before washing his hands and feet. Then he and his companions drank from the water that he had blessed."[78] Commenting further on the outcomes of Columba's actions, Adomnan adds, "Since that day, the demons have kept away from

76. Irvin and Sunquist, *History of the World Christian Movement*, 226.

77. Severus, *Life of Martin* 15 cited in Blocher and Blandenier, *Evangelization of the World*, 45.

78. Adomnan, *Life of Columba* 2.11 (all translations are from Sharpe).

the well. Instead, far from harming anyone, after the saint had blessed it and washed in it, many ailments among the local people were cured by that well."[79] In this account, we observe an interesting combination of both power encounter and healing as demons are cast out of the well and the Picts are no longer made sick by the water. In addition, the water apparently acquired healing qualities.

In another account of healing, Adomnan notes that following the conversion of a Pictish man and his family, his son fell sick and died. As the family was being mocked by pagan religious leaders, Columba was called to the home. Adomnan adds:

> Seeing their great distress, St. Columba comforted [the family] and assured them that they should not in any way doubt that God is almighty . . . Having gone inside, St. Columba immediately knelt and, with tears streaming down his face, prayed to Christ the Lord. After these prayers on bended knee, he stood up and turned his gaze to the dead boy, saying: "In the name of the Lord Jesus Christ, wake up again and stand upon thy feet." At the saint's glorious word, the soul returned to the body, and the boy that was dead opened his eyes and lived again . . . He gave the boy, now restored to life, back to his parents, and a great shout went up from the crowd.[80]

Columba's biographer concludes by showing that this power encounter, marked by evangelical proclamation, resulted in more Pictish people embracing the gospel. Adomnan concludes: "Mourning gave way to celebration and the God of the Christians was glorified."[81]

Conclusion

In this chapter, the argument has been made that early Christian mission—not unlike the ministry of Jesus—was characterized by ministry in Word and deed. That is, mission was not isolated to proclamation alone; nor did mission ever become gospel-less humanitarian aid. While we observe that the gospel message—centered around the death, burial, and resurrection of Christ and supported by the rule of faith and early Christian

79. Ibid.
80. Ibid., 2.32.
81. Ibid.

creeds—remained unchanged, there was some diversity in deed ministry. It has been argued that in its mission, the church cared for the poor, hungry, imprisoned, enslaved and otherwise marginalized. Yet, I have also asserted that deed ministry could be observed through miracles and power encounters.

What conclusions can be drawn from this discussion? First, because of the centrality of the gospel in the ministry of Gregory Thaumaturgus, Martin, Columba and others, their reported miracles and power encounters did not turn Christianity into another form of magic. Rather, these actions served as a sign to give credence to the message being proclaimed. Put another way, power encounters routinely translated into truth encounters.

Second, unlike today, there was little debate in the church over the relationship between proclamation and social action. Indeed, the bifurcation of the two areas and the response by way of the holism-prioritism debate are truly reflections of late nineteenth- and early twentieth-century developments in the church in the West. While Basil comes the closest to stating that proclamation has priority, the rest of the testimony of early Christian mission appears rather silent. Does this mean that evangelism and social action were equal partners? I don't think so. Instead, I suggest that missionaries in the early church were quite gospel-driven; yet, as they moved out in mission and proclaimed the good news, they intuitively cared for other needs (e.g., poverty, demon possession) as they arose. Is this how they defined mission? Again, I don't think so because we hardly hear the word mission used in the early church, much less hear debate on the contours of its meaning. In summary, as the early church was on mission, its representatives imitated Jesus in caring for the poor, sick, marginalized, and demon-possessed while proclaiming life in his name.

Questions for Reflection

1. Read Mark 1:21–28:

   And they went into Capernaum, and immediately on the Sabbath he entered the synagogue and was teaching. And they were astonished at his teaching, for he taught them as one who had authority, and not as the scribes. And immediately there was in their synagogue a man with an unclean spirit. And he cried out, "What have you to do with us, Jesus of Nazareth? Have you come to destroy us? I know who you are—the Holy One of God." But Jesus rebuked him, saying, "Be silent, and come out of him!" And the unclean spirit, convulsing him and crying out with a loud voice, came out of him. And they were all amazed, so that they questioned among themselves, saying, "What is this? A new teaching with authority! He commands even the unclean spirits, and they obey him." And at once his fame spread everywhere throughout all the surrounding region of Galilee.

   How would Justin Martyr or Columba read and interpret this passage differently than many modern students and scholars of Scripture?

2. What can modern Christians learn from the early church about the spiritual world and miracles, especially as it relates to mission?

3. What do the monastic vales of prayer and labor or contemplation and activism teach us about ministering the gospel in Word and in deed?

4. What elements of Basil's "new city" *(basileas)* approach could be recovered and used in ministry today?

5. From this survey of Word and deed ministry in the early church, how would you describe the relationship between evangelism and caring for human needs?

8

Church

IN MATTHEW 16:18, JUST ONE of two references to the term church in the Gospels, the evangelist remembers Jesus declaring to Peter, "I will build my church and the gates of hell shall not prevail against it." Though this is an often debated passage between Roman Catholics and Protestants over Peter's role and authority in the church, the promise remains clear that church planting and growth is the work of Christ who serves as its head. Later in Acts, Luke describes a recently planted church in Antioch deliberately engaged in missions sending: "Now there were in the church at Antioch prophets and teachers, Barnabas, Simeon who was called Niger, Lucius of Cyrene, Manaen a lifelong friend of Herod the tetrarch, and Saul. While they were worshiping the Lord and fasting, the Holy Spirit said, 'Set apart for me Barnabas and Saul for the work to which I have called them.' Then after fasting and praying they laid their hands on them and sent them off."[1] Commenting on the Antioch church's actions, I. Howard Marshall writes, "The picture is of a local church taking the responsibility for sending out missionaries who remain in touch with it and return at the end of their mission."[2] Indeed, the most visible outcome of the ministry of Jesus and his earliest followers was the church—the *ecclesia* or "called out" ones who assembled together to worship, teach the Scriptures, fellowship, and to be on mission.

1. Acts 13:1–3.
2. Marshall, "Who Were the Evangelists?," 258.

Church planting was also central to the work of the Apostle Paul. In his early twentieth-century seminal work, *Missionary Methods: St. Paul's or Ours?*, Roland Allen asserted, "St. Paul did not gather congregations, he planted churches, and he did not leave a church until it was fully equipped with orders of ministry, sacraments, and tradition."[3] Marshall adds that Paul was quite pleased that newly planted congregations were also involved in their own missions activity.[4] Allen further argues that church planting should not be regarded as something unique to Paul's missionary work; instead, it represented a viable biblical model for mission. He writes that Paul's work "was really intended to throw light on the path of those who should come after."[5]

In short, mission in the New Testament was necessarily church-centered. On one hand, the church was the product of mission; on the other, it was also the means for it. As the gospel spread in the early Christian world, especially in the absence of buildings and clerical hierarchies, a spontaneous multiplication of churches could be observed. In this chapter, our task is to focus on the church in early Christian mission by considering how the church embodied and embraced mission. Our study is necessarily broken into two main periods: from the first to early fourth centuries when churches largely met in homes, and then from the fourth century onward when communities began to gather in public basilicas. Though a distinction is made between these two periods, we will still show that church-centered mission could be observed even after Constantine gave peace to the church in the Roman Empire. With our focus limited to the question of church and mission, I will not go into significant detail on subjects such as church leadership structures, ecclesiology, household codes in the Roman world, and early Christian architecture.

House Churches

Del Birkey insightfully writes, "If you had asked another for directions to a church in any important city of the first-century world, you would have been directed to somebody's private home!"[6] Though the earliest followers of Jesus were Jews, their commitment to the death, burial, and resurrection

3. Allen, *Missionary Methods,* Kindle Locations, 92–93.

4. Marshall, "Who were the Evangelists?," 259, 262.

5. Allen, *Missionary Methods*, Kindle Location 66.

6. Birkey, *House Church*, 40.

of the Messiah made it difficult for them to continue worshipping in the synagogue, which resulted in Christian worship taking place in homes.[7] Hvalvik correctly adds that "such gatherings took place in private houses of the more well-to-do members of the congregation."[8] While at times, suffering churches met in secret—such as the third-century church in Gaul meeting in a *labitula* ("hole")—for the most part, early Christians prior to Constantine gathered in homes.[9]

Though the early Christian movement was regarded as an illegal sect (*religio illicita*) during much of the first four centuries, house churches in the Roman context were quite public. This was largely due to the fact that Roman villas were already built in an open manner reflecting the Roman ideal that a house should be a semi-public space. Clarke affirms that "the Roman house was in no way private. It was the locus of the owner's social, political, and business activities, open both to invited and uninvited visitors."[10] While some wealthier Christians opened their homes for Christian worship—gatherings that probably included thirty to forty people—house groups also met in more modest accommodations as well. This continual need for meeting space was certainly due to the rapid expansion of the early church. Hvalvik notes that many Romans, possibly as high as 90 percent of the people, lived in *insulae*: "apartment buildings with three or more floors reaching up to twenty meters."[11] These gatherings were probably less private than those held in private villas because, as Hvalvik adds, "In such a location a Christian meeting could not possibly take place without the knowledge of everybody else in the building."[12]

Summarizing the nature of early Christian meeting spaces, Gehring writes: "For nearly three hundred years—until the fourth century, when Constantine began building the first basilicas throughout the Roman Empire—Christians gathered in private houses built initially for domestic use, not in church buildings originally constructed for the sole purpose of public

---

7. Irvin and Sunquist, *History of the World Christian Movement*, 26; also Gehring, *House Church and Mission*, 30, 73–74.

8. Hvalvik, "Word and Deed," 281.

9. Thomas, *Christianity in Roman Britain*, 155.

10. Cited in Hvalvik, "Word and Deed," 281; cf. Osiek and Balch, *Families in the New Testament World*, 17, 24, 44.

11. Hvalvik, "Word and Deed," 282; also Osiek and Blach, *Families in the New Testament World*, 11–12, 20–24, 31.

12. Hvalvik, "Word and Deed," 282.

worship."[13] Irvin and Sunquist note, however, that public church buildings began to be constructed as early as the third century.[14] In resolving this apparent contradiction, it should be noted that while Constantine's actions toward the church did serve as a radical shift, the transition from churches meeting in private homes to public basilicas was actually a gradual one over time as the needs of the Christian communities changed. Summarizing the consensus of scholarship, Gehring captures this architectural progression in three major steps:

> (a) The *house church* was defined as a private house that remained architecturally unaltered. This house was used by a local Christian group for public worship and by the owner (and his/her family) for private domestic purposes. (b) A *church house* (... *domus ecclesiae*) is a private domestic house that was physically altered and adapted in order to meet the social and/or religious needs of the group ... (c) a *hall church* (their *aula ecclesiae*) refers to a larger, more formal, rectangular (private or public) hall that was used by Christians exclusively for social and religious purposes.[15]

Instead of asserting that church buildings were being constructed from the ground up in the third century, the better argument is that existing private homes were being modified into church houses for the needs of the expanding community.

The most well-known excavated church facility from the third century—at Dura Europas in Mesopotamia—provides a good example of a *domus ecclesiae*.[16] Following two pages of diagrams that show the building's transformation from private home to church house, Birkey comments, "Before it was adapted for a Christian meeting place, the house consisted of eight rooms and a courtyard ... Somewhere between AD 232 and AD 256, the house was altered for use as a gathering place for Christians, adding a baptistery and wall paintings." [17] Though Birkey argues that the church house retained some aspects of privacy because it was located among other villas, Gehring correctly asserts that such construction on this and other

---

13. Ibid., 1.

14. Irvin and Sunquist, *History of the World Christian Movement*, 99.

15. Gehring, *House Church and Mission*, 18–19; cf. Osiek and Balch, *Families in the New Testament World*, 214.

16. Irvin and Sunquist, *History of the World Christian Movement*, 54; Osiek and Blach, *Families in the New Testament World*, 35; cf. Frend, *Martyrdom and Persecution*, 228–29.

17. Birkey, *House Church*, 55.

early church facilities only invited more attention from the community to what was an already public structure.[18]

Figure 10: Mosaic of North African converted house.

Given these architectural considerations, what was the significance for the house (*oikos*) structure of the ancient world, especially in light of Christian mission? Simply put, the household, comprised of multiple nuclear families, was the "*the* basic social and economic form not only for the ancient world and the New Testament but presumably for every pre-industrial sedentary culture as well."[19] Gehring adds that "Scarcely anything determined daily life more than the *oikos* with its network of relationships. It was an all-encompassing social structure with legal, economic, and biological implications."[20] On a relational level, the *oikos* structure mirrored the open architecture of the Roman villa, which facilitated new and existing relationships. The fact that the terms *oikos* (family) and *domus* (house) were used interchangeably support this social reality.[21] It should be noted

18. Ibid., 55; Gehring, *House Church and Mission*, 290.

19. Luhrman cited in Ibid., 17; cf. Birkey, *House Church*, 38.

20. Gehring, *House Church and Mission*, 17.

21. Osiek and Balch, *Families in the New Testament World*, 6.

that in the Roman context the household was also the center of religious life and the place for pagan sacrifices.[22] Gehring concludes that "the significance of the *oikos* for the establishment and organization of early Christian church life can hardly be overemphasized,"[23] while Hvalvik adds, "The early Christians were part of families and other social networks . . . this became a most important factor in the spreading of the Christian faith."[24]

Though the household network was strategic for mission for these social and cultural reasons, there is further precedent for deliberate house-based mission in the first century, which may have shaped how later Christian households thought about church and mission. In the ministry of Jesus, Peter's house in Capernaum served as a strategic base for the Lord's work in the region, while the Galilean mission was accomplished through a house to house approach.[25] Affirming that Jesus' disciples followed this model, Gehring writes: "Missional outreach began with a house, that is, with a family, which probably meant with the head of the household . . . It spread from there in ever larger circles, reaching its climax once the entire town had been exposed to the message of the coming kingdom."[26] The Jerusalem church also demonstrated these values as Christian homes were places where the gathered community could enjoy a collective witness and where gospel-focused conversations took place.[27]

House churches were also central to Paul's mission. A cursory reading of Acts and the Pauline epistles show that house churches were the most visible outcome of Paul's missionary labors.[28] In addition to these homes being centers for fellowship, worship, and teaching, they were also places where leaders could be trained and set apart. Often, heads of houses provided hospitality and financial assistance for the community and became the natural leader for those that met in their homes.[29] Gehring adds that "the house with its workshop and its network of relationships . . . offer[ed]

22. Kalantzis, *Caesar and the Lamb*, 19.

23. Gehring, *House Church and Mission*, 17.

24. Hvalvik, "Word and Deed," 282.

25. Gehring, *House Church and Mission*, 38–46; Osiek and Balch, *Families in the New Testament World*, 32–33.

26. Gehring, *House Church and Mission*, 54.

27. Ibid., 91–95, 116–17.

28. Ibid., 119–35; also Birkey, *House Church*, 40–55.

29. Gehring, *House Church and Mission*, 180; also Osiek and Blach, *Families in the New Testament World*, 38–39, 214.

natural evangelistic contacts and conversation opportunities."[30] That is, the house church was also a center for mission.

Given this survey of the house church phenomenon, let us briefly summarize the missional implications for house churches. First, culturally, the *oikos* structure was understood by the ancient world and a relevant social network. As a result, it was not only a place where authentic worship and fellowship could take place, but it was a meaningful environment in which to assimilate new believers in Christ. Further, it was a place where biblical hospitality could be practiced and demonstrated—a sign of authentic fellowship among Christians that also served as a collective witness to non-believing guests.[31] As noted, the burden of hospitality fell largely on the head of the household who often became the leader of that local gathering. Not surprisingly, the Pastoral Epistles included hospitality as one of the requirements for a church leader.[32] Finally, the house church—as the family of God (*familia Dei*) and house of God (*oikos theou*)—served to transform some aspects of culture that were counter to the gospel as rich and poor, men and women, and slaves and free people became a family in Christ.[33] In short, as the *oikos* structure was a natural medium for social networking in the ancient world and with the deliberate emphases by Jesus and Paul to minister from house to house, the house church model was central to mission strategy through the early fourth century. Even when we think about large Christian communities such as those at Rome, Carthage, and Antioch, we must envision a network of house churches.

The Essence of the Church

After a number of years of laboring as a church planter in France with very little fruit and quite a bit of discouragement, Brethren church planter Tom Julien retreated and asked the basic, perplexing question, "what is a local church?"[34] Acknowledging that most missionaries "identify the local church by her cultural and historic expression," Julien began a quest to understand the church through "her biblical essence."[35] After studying the New Testament, Julien became convinced that "the essence of the church

30. Gehring, *House Church and* Mission, 181.

31. Ibid., 293; also Osiek and Balch, *Families in the New Testament World*, 39, 210–14; cf. Riddle, "Early Christian Hospitality," 141–54.

32. 1 Tim 3:2; Titus 1:8.

33. Gehring, *House Church and* Mission, 294.

34. Julien, "Essence of the Church."

35. Ibid.

> *(continued)*
>
> is revealed mainly in images," including things like a "spiritual building," "the spiritual body," and "the spiritual body," and "the bride, the vine, and the flock."[36] Julien summarizes, "In each of these images, the dominant factor is the intimate union between Christ and the believer. Yet, most attempts to define the local church ignore the Head altogether. We must not define the church from the neck down; she has a Head."[37] Having stripped down the notion of church to its bare biblical essentials, Julien and his wife re-launched their ministry in France with renewed hope to see this essence manifest itself in a French context. As they labored with greater apparent success, they presented an important model for thinking biblically about church and avoiding importing expressions and forms from outside cultures.

Basilicas and Mission

As discussed, the transition from house churches to public basilicas was a gradual one. Although Constantine began to commission the building of public church spaces in the fourth century,[38] it is interesting to note that many public meeting places around the Roman world were converted private homes. For instance, in Gaul a senator's house was converted into a church building around 333. Thomas adds: "As we look around at northern Gaul and the great valleys of the Rhine and the Mosel; a good many churches known to begin in the early fifth century apparently originated in such acquisitions and conversions."[39]

The transition to basilicas in Roman Britain occurred even more slowly. In fact, Thomas argues that such structures did not exist in Britain until 425, over a century after Constantine's rise to power.[40] Though there is evidence for bishops in the British church since the early fourth century, these leaders probably convened worship and led the church through modified homes. In light of this, the notion of church was certainly not tied to a building or location. Thomas adds further: "At least until the fifth century, British Latin exhibited a certain looseness in finding any one specific word to mean 'a Christian church building.' The range of terms used very

36. Ibid; cf. Guder, *Missional Church*, 13–14.
37. Julien, "Essence of the Church."
38. Deckers, "Constantine the Great and Early Christian Art," 92–93.
39. Thomas, *Christianity in Roman Britain*, 156.
40. Ibid., 147–49.

probably did include *ecclesia* (though we have no early example); but the assumption that *ecclesia* necessarily and exclusively meant 'a church building' rather than ... 'a Christian congregation,' is unsound."[41] Interestingly, when Patrick of Ireland spoke of *ecclesia,* he did not refer to a building or even a local congregation of believers, but rather the universal church. Perhaps Patrick's missional convictions caused him to think about the church in less institutional and structural terms. As a whole, it seems that British ecclesiology was not overly influenced by buildings through the fifth century.[42]

As basilicas were being constructed around the Roman world, what values guided this process? Summarizing the worship needs that the basilica structure facilitated, Wilken writes: "Christian worship required a large interior space where people could gather, a podium, called an ambo, at which the Scriptures could be read, a table or altar, where the vessels holding the bread and wine could be placed and ample space for movement of the clergy and the people. There were no seats in the early churches, and people stood during worship."[43] As shown, because of conflict with both Jewish and Roman authorities, the earliest Christians ceased from worshipping in synagogues and opted for meeting in homes. However, once peace was accorded to the church, the Christians chose not to revert to a synagogue-style structure; rather, they chose the basilica—a multi-purpose building already common in Roman society.[44] Such a structure facilitated the needs of the congregation—including worship, fellowship, and even mission to the community.[45]

One concrete way that some Roman basilicas facilitated mission and gospel proclamation was through the art[46]—paintings, mosaics, and stone carvings—that adorned their walls, ceilings, floors, and even doors.[47] This is most apparent from the fourth century onward when basilica construction began to accelerate.[48] Though some scholarly attention has been given

41. Ibid., 149.

42. Ibid., 149–55.

43. Wilken, *First Thousand Years,* 137.

44. Deckers, "Constantine the Great and Early Christian Art," 93–94.

45. Ibid., 137.

46. For more in depth studies of early Christian art, see Jensen, *Understanding Early Christian Art*; Jensen, "Early Christian Images and Exegesis"; Jensen, "Material Evidence (2)"; and Spier, *Picturing the Bible.*

47. Kessler, "Bright Gardens of Paradise," 116–38.

48. Jensen, *Understanding Early Christian Art,* 15–16; Jensen, "Early Christian Images and Exegesis," 72.

to the relationship between early Christian art, theology, and hermeneutics, there has been less discussion on how church art aided gospel proclamation. Some insights can be gleaned from Bishop Gregory of Rome who chastised a church leader for destroying some icons: "what writing presents to readers, a picture presents to the unlearned who view it, since in the image even the ignorant see what they ought to follow; in the picture the illiterate read."[49] While it may be argued that Gregory was referring to visual imagery helping illiterate Christians, we should remember that this is the same missions-minded bishop who sent Augustine of Canterbury and a team of monks to England in the late sixth century. So Gregory's sentiments could have also applied to non-believing visitors to the church. It should be noted that the illiterate were not the only ones to benefit from church art; those who could read could also visualize the gospel from such works as well.

**Figure 11: Sufetula (Sbeitla, Tunisia) baptistery
(copyright © Marcus Brooks; used with permission).**

49. Gregory, *Letter* 13 cited in Jensen, *Understanding Early Christian Art*, 3.

What characterized basilica art in this period? Wilken helpfully writes: "Christian art tends toward narrative, the telling of a story, the depiction of events from biblical history . . . so it was to this history, and the persons and events who appear in the biblical stories that Christians turned when they wished to decorate their churches."[50] Jensen adds that church images were especially concerned with conveying a complete narrative; not merely a single figure or element of a story.[51] For example, a number of Old Testament stories were regularly depicted in basilicas including the accounts of Adam and Eve, Abraham attempting to sacrifice Isaac, Noah and the Ark, and Jonah's journey to Nineveh.[52] However, central to the message of Christian art was the person and work of Christ and basilica walls contained images of the Lord being visited by the magi as a baby, entering Jerusalem before the passion week, and washing his disciples' feet. Further, the essence of Christ's saving work—his suffering, death on the cross, burial, and resurrection—was also captured. Jensen asserts that "fourth-century portrayals of the passion story that include scenes of Jesus' arrest, trial, and his carrying the cross . . . are all tied to recognizable episodes from the Gospels."[53] Emphasizing further the continuity between what was preached, read, and observed visually within a basilica, Jensen adds, "Visual representations of Jesus, together with theological treatises, homilies, and apologies, helped establish and declare publicly what Christians believed about him."[54]

In cataloging the art in one fifth-century basilica, Deckers likens the fifth-century Christian's walk to the altar at the front of the church to a visual journey through the narrative of Scripture. He writes: "The pictorial cycles on the walls above . . . told of God's plan for salvation, anticipated in many stages over the centuries and culminating . . . in the appearance of Christ and his apostles. With the aid of these pictures, the believer could retrace spiritually the realization of that holy plan on the way to the altar, where, by lifting his gaze, he could see in the crown of the apse the image of the eternal, omnipotent Christ."[55] To be sure, this experience served as a reminder to Christians about their hope in Christ; however, it seems that

50. Wilken, *First Thousand Years*, 140–41.

51. Jensen, "Early Christian Images," 68.

52. Spier, *Picturing the Bible*, 206–88.

53. Jensen, *Understanding Early Christian Art*, 130.

54. Ibid., 102.

55. Deckers, "Constantine the Great and Early Christian Art," 99.

such basilica art offered a chance for non-believers to see and grasp the gospel as well.

Church-Based Mission

Though since the earliest Christian period, missionaries were sent out from established churches to proclaim the gospel, evangelism continued to happen within the context of the church. While monastic missionary societies such as the Franciscans and Dominicans would emerge in the medieval period, one defining attribute of early Christian mission was that the church itself was a viable locus of mission.

As discussed, Basil of Caesarea's ministry in Asia Minor, was characterized by church-based mission. Inspired by Gregory Thaumaturgus who had evangelized third-century Cappadocia through his preaching, Basil shared Gregory's evangelistic conviction.[56] Probably valuing proclamation as the most important element of his ministry, Basil preached to nourish the faithful but also evangelize non-believers visiting the church.[57]

By the fourth century, church fathers such as Ambrose of Milan and Augustine of Hippo communicated the call to salvation in Christ by inviting non-believers to put in their names for baptism. This invitation was especially given after Christmas as the church worshipped through the period of Lent toward Easter—the traditional time for baptism. Let us briefly examine the progression of early Christian catechesis and how it effectively blurred the lines between evangelism and discipleship within the context of the church.[58]

After submitting their names, petitioners were scrutinized by the church leadership and, if accepted, they were admitted as catechumens— those preparing for baptism.[59] From the early second century, there is evidence that instruction was given prior to baptism. In the early third century, Hippolytus (ca. 170–236) in his *Apostolic Tradition*, referred to

56. Sterk, *Renouncing the World Yet Leading the Church*, 37; Basil, *On the Holy Spirit*, 29.34.

57. Basil, *Morals* 70.9–11, 31–34.

58. This chapter's discussion on catechesis, community evangelism, and testimonies is based on my previous article, Smither, "Reflections on Patristic Evangelism and Discipleship." See also Kreider, *Change of Conversion*, 21–32.

59. This term developed in the third century and was used in *Passion of Perpetua and Felicitas* 2; and Tertullian, *Prescription against Heretics* 41; see also Yarnold, *Awe-Inspiring Rites of Initiation*, 2–6.

a fairly developed system of catechesis in Rome that included three years of pre-baptismal teaching. In the fourth century, the catechumenate was largely confined to the forty-day Lenten period leading up to Easter.[60]

What was the content of a catechumen's instruction? New believers, many of whom came from pagan backgrounds, were provided with moral instruction from the Scriptures.[61] At the same time, they were exorcized and invited to renounce their former life. At various stages in the early church period, exorcism took place at the outset of the catechumenate, during Lent, and just prior to baptism.[62] Irenaeus and Augustine both included a survey of biblical and salvation history in their catechesis.[63] Eventually, the focal point of pre-baptismal catechetical instruction became the Nicene Creed. During the Lenten period, catechumens received lectures in which each line of the Creed was expounded and then, just prior to baptism, they "handed it back" (*traditio*) in a public declaration of faith. In some communities, the Lord's Prayer was also recited in a similar manner. In the week following baptism, further instruction was given on the meaning of baptism, chrism (anointing with oil), and the Eucharist.[64]

Given the significant number of treatises and sermons devoted to catechesis in the patristic period, including manuals written to train and equip catechists, it is quite evident that teaching new believers both before and after baptism was a priority for the early church.[65] What were the prevailing discipleship values for catechumens? First, the church recognized

60. *Didache* 7.1; Justin, *First Apology* 61; also Ferguson, "Catechesis, Catechumenate," 223. Hyppolytus, *Apostolic Tradition* 17.1.

61. For a thorough discussion of each stage of the catechumenate, including baptism, see Yarnold, *Awe-Inspiring Rites of Initiation*, 2–40; see also *Didache* 1–6; Justin, *First Apology* 61.

62. Yarnold, *Awe-Inspiring Rites of Initiation*, 5, 9, 18–20.

63. See Irenaeus, *Proof of the Apostolic Preaching*; and Augustine, *Instructing Beginners in Faith*.

64. Yarnold, *Awe-Inspiring Rites of Initiation*, 12–14; also Ferguson, "Catechesis, Catechumenate," 224.

65. Though my discussion has primarily dealt with catechesis in the western church, the following sermons and treatises on catechesis show a rich catechetical tradition in the western and eastern church: Irenaeus, *Proof of the Apostolic Preaching*; Hippolytus, *Apostolic Tradition* 16–20; Cyril of Jerusalem, *Catechetical Lectures*; author unknown, *Mystagogical Catecheses*; Theodore of Mopsuestia, *Catechetical Homilies*; John Chrysostom, *Baptismal Catecheses*; Ambrose, *On the Mysteries, On the Sacraments*, and *Explanation of the Symbol*; and Augustine, *Sermons* 56–59, 212–18, 363. Training guides and manuals for catechists included: Gregory of Nyssa, *Catechetical Orations*; and Augustine, *Instructing Beginners in Faith* and *On Faith and the Creed*.

that many came from pagan backgrounds and had much to learn about the gospel and much to change in their lives. The emphasis on exorcism also reveals a worldview that acknowledged the presence and work of the Evil One. Hence, with conversion, the new believer also had a great deal to renounce from the former life.[66]

Second, and related, there was significant emphasis on moral and character change. Perhaps the *Didache's* emphasis on choosing the "way of life" over the "way of death" best communicates this value.[67] Though he spoke of a three-year catechumenate in his *Apostolic Tradition*, Hippolytus indicated that the most important consideration was whether the catechumen had experienced life change: "Have they honored the widows? Have they visited the sick? Have they done every kind of good work?" In this case, "the time shall not be judged, but only [the candidate's] conduct."[68]

Third, there was an emphasis on sound doctrine and Scripture. As noted, every believer needed to be able to hand over the Creed prior to being baptized and Irenaeus and Augustine included a survey of biblical and salvation history as part of their teaching. Scripture's importance did not diminish at the end of the catechumenate as the reading and preaching of Scripture occupied a central place in communal worship in the early Christian period.

Finally, the process of the catechumenate also pointed to the sanctity of worship. Catechumens as well as non-believers were dismissed from the worship assembly before the Eucharist was celebrated. This opportunity for worship was reserved for those who had shown themselves faithful to learn the Scriptures and the Creed, to declare their faith publicly in baptism, and thus to appreciate the importance of corporate worship in the community of believers.

Celtic Church Leadership Structures

While much attention has already been given to this point on Celtic monastic missions, one final observation is that the movement's missionary

66. See Justin, *First Apology* 14; Augustine, *Sermon* 215.1; also Merdinger, "Do You Renounce Satan and All His Works?"; and Kreider, "'They Alone Know the Right Way to Live,'" 177.

67. *Didache* 1–6; also Ferguson, "Catechesis, Catechumenate," 223.

68. Hippolytus, *Apostolic Tradition* 19, 17, cited in Kreider, "'They Alone Know the Right Way to Live,'" 176.

monastic ethos seems to have affected the leadership structure of the Irish church. We recall that one of Ireland's early missionary pioneers, Patrick, was set apart as a missionary-monk-bishop by Celestine of Rome and then by the British church to evangelize the Irish.[69] Blocher and Blandenier note, "The Irish church slowly developed its own structure that followed the monastic form. Parishes were directed by communities of monks, with the abbey's authority soon supplanting the bishop's."[70] It seems that the same monastic structure that facilitated its missionary efforts was adopted to lead the established church—one that was a leader in missions-sending in Europe in the sixth and seventh centuries. Interestingly, the Celtic church later experienced conflict with the rest of the church in Britain, which had adopted a more Roman style of leadership.[71]

Conclusion

In this chapter, I have argued that church was central to mission in the early Christian centuries—both before and after Constantine. Though mission strategies changed over time and church forms looked different, there was never a time when there was church-less Christianity. The most visible expression of Christian mission was the church and the most powerful means for it was the church. In the first century, mission was accomplished through a deliberate house-to-house approach, while the *oikos* structure facilitated an organic church especially during periods of time when Christians were unable to exist as a legitimate organization.

Even after peace was given to the church, mission flowed from the church and back to the church, especially in the absence of missionary orders and societies. That evangelism, catechesis, and baptism efforts were located in the context of the church solidified this church-focused mission. In addition, the ministries of Cyprian, Martin of Tours, Athanasius, Basil and Augustine to evangelize heretics could also be understood in light of the church's ongoing commitment to evangelize itself. Our discussion of church art showed that non-believers could embrace the gospel through seeing the gospel visually in basilicas built after the fourth century. Though the public acceptance of Christianity and the construction of buildings probably thwarted the spontaneous multiplication of churches that the

69. Hunter, *Celtic Way of Evangelism*, 15.

70. Blocher and Blandenier, *Evangelization of the World*, 60.

71. Ibid., 61.

house churches facilitated, there is still a sense of mission in the period of our study and the church remains a central element.

Questions for Reflection

1. Read 1 Corinthians 16: 19–20: The churches of Asia send you greetings. Aquila and Prisca, together with the church in their house, send you hearty greetings in the Lord. All the brothers send you greetings.

   How did first-century households facilitate Christian mission?

2. What would a missional house church approach look like today? In the western and non-western world? In free countries and in contexts where there is no freedom of religion?

3. How was Christian mission affected by the rise of Constantine and the building of basilicas?

4. What does it mean to evangelize the church today in your context?

Epilogue

MY HOPE AND PRAYER IS that this book will continue a conversation about what can be learned today from the early church's experience in mission. Certainly, when we gaze at the history of missions, we encounter what is familiar and also what is strange. When Basil cares for the poor, Mesrop translates Scripture, or when monks proclaim the death, burial, and resurrection of Christ, we feel right at home. On the other hand, when Columba approaches the palace before the people with the gospel, when Martin of Tours destroys pagan temples, or even when many accounts attest to the miraculous, modern Christians might feel a bit uncomfortable. The aim in these pages has been to sketch out some of the more prominent themes of early Christian mission and lay them out before the reader to begin a reflective conversation. What did the early church do well? What can we emulate today? What should we leave in the past? Above all, my hope is that what we learn from mission in the early church will drive us back into pages of Scripture to make sense of our history, ourselves, and how we ought to be thinking about and approaching mission.

Indeed, there is much more that can be explored—geographic regions, social and cultural contexts, mission strategies, church movements, and what the early church believed about mission. I believe that each chapter could be expanded into an entire book. For instance, I could envision a single work on how early Christian missionaries engaged political leaders and how authentic mission continued after peace was given to the church. Also, I think much more research is needed into the history and theology of missionary monks. Certainly, more study on how the church engaged other religions (e.g., Islam, Zoroastrianism, and Buddhism) would also be very helpful.

While there is much more to be studied—even elements of our history that are "messy" and troubling—I am confident that this book has made one thing clear: that the church has never been without its mission. Indeed, in each period as God's people have read the Scriptures, the church has been reminded of its place in the *missio Dei*. Despite the declarations of some monarchs making Christianity the national or imperial religion, gospel proclamation and the expansion of the church never ceased. My evangelical brothers and sisters ought to be reassured that there was much winsome mission activity after the Apostle Paul and before William Carey. While it is good for evangelicals to acknowledge many of the good things of pre-Reformation church history, it is also good for scholars of early Christianity to give more regard to the mission of the church as a framework for historical studies.

Finally, this study has reminded me once again that the church of Jesus Christ has a memory. In this case, it is a missional memory—an account of the gospel and how it advanced across barriers of geography, culture, and belief through the devoted work of monks, merchants, bishops, and others who believed that the message was so important that they would leave their homes, families, and all that was familiar in order to proclaim the gospel. It is good to reflect on the church's memory of mission and consider how it might shape us today.

Bibliography

Ackroyd, P. R., and C. F. Evans, eds. *The Cambridge History of the Bible*, Vol. 1, *From the Beginnings to Jerome*. Cambridge: Cambridge University Press, 1970, 1989.

"Ad Scapulum." *The Tertullian Project*. Online: http://www.tertullian.org/works/ad_scapulam.htm/.

Admonan. *Life of St. Columba*. Translated by Richard Sharpe. London: Penguin, 1995.

Adna, Jostein, and Hans Kvalbein, eds. *The Mission of the Early Church to Jews and Gentiles*. Wissenschaftliche Untersuchungen zum Neuen Testament 127. Tübingen: Mohr/Siebeck, 2000.

Agathangelos. "History of the Armenians." In *Readings in World Christian History*, Vol. 1, *Earliest Christianity to 1453*, edited by John W. Coakley and Andrea Sterk, 122–30. Maryknoll, NY: Orbis, 2004.

Alexander, David. *Augustine's Early Theology of the Church: Emergence and Implications, 386–91*. New York: Lang, 2008.

Allen, Roland. *Missionary Methods: St. Paul's or Ours?* GLH. Kindle ed., 2011.

"Apologeticum." *The Tertullian Project*. Online: http://www.tertullian.org/works/apologeticum.htm/.

The Armenian Church. Online: http://www.armenianchurch-ed.net/our-church/history-of-the-church/history/.

Athanasius, *Letter 39*. In *NPNF* 2:4. Online: http://www.ccel.org/ccel/schaff/npnf204.xxv.iii.iii.xxv.html/.

Augustine. Saint. *Arianism and Other Heresies*. Works of Saint Augustine: A Translation for the 21st Century, part 1, vol. 18. Hyde Park, NY: New City, 1995.

———. Confessions. *Works of Saint Augustine: A Translation for the 21st Century*. Translated by Maria Boulding. Hyde Park, NY: New City, 1997.

———. *Letters*. Works of Saint Augustine: A Translation for the 21st Century. ed. John E. Rotelle. Volume 2, books 1–4, Hyde Park, NY: New City Press, 2001–2005.

———. *Sermons*. Works of Saint Augustine: A Translation for the 21st Century, ed. John E. Rotelle, Volume III, books 1–11. Hyde Park, NY: New City, 1994.

———. *Teaching Christianity*. Works of Saint Augustine: A Translation for the 21st Century. Translated by Edmund Hill. Hyde Park, NY: New City, 1996.

Auxentius of Durostorum. *Letter on the Life and Work of Ulfila, Apostle of the Goths*. In *Readings in World Christianity. Volume I, Earliest Christianity to 1453*, edited by John W. Coakley and Andrea Sterk, 102–5. Maryknoll, NY: Orbis, 2004.

Baarda, Tjitze. *Essays on the Diatessaron*. Contributions to Biblical Exegesis and Theology 11. Kampen: Kok Pharos, 1994.

Barnes, Timothy D. *Constantine and Eusebius*. Cambridge: Harvard Univesity Press, 1981.

Basil of Caesarea, Saint. *Letters, Volume 1 (1–185)*. FC 13. Translated by Agnes Clare Way. Washington, DC: Catholic University Press, 1951.

————. *Letters, Volume 2 (186–368),* Fathers of the Church 28. Translated by Agnes Clare Way. Washington DC: Catholic University Press, 1955.

————. *Long Rules, Short Rules, Morals. Saint Basil's Ascetical Works, Fathers of the Church* 5. Translated by M. Monica Wagner. Washington, DC: Catholic University Press, 1962.

————. *On the Holy Spirit.* Translated by David Anderson. Crestwood, NY: St. Vladimir's Seminary Press, 1980.

Bede, the Venerable, Saint. *Ecclesiastical History of the English People; The Greater Chronicle; Bede's Letter to Egbert.* Translated by Judith McClure and Roger Collins. Oxford: Oxford University Press, 1994, 2008.

Bevans, Stephen B., and Schroeder, Roger P. *Constants in Context: A Theology of Mission for Today.* Maryknoll, NY: Orbis, 2008.

Birdsall, J. N. "The New Testament Text." In *From the Beginnings to Jerome,* edited by P. R. Ackroyd and C. F. Evans, 308–76. The Cambridge History of the Bible 1. Cambridge: Cambridge University Press, 1970, 1989.

Birkey, Del. *The House Church: A Model for Renewing the Church.* Scottdale, PA: Herald, 1988.

Brent, Allen. *A Political History of Early Christianity.* London: T. & T. Clark, 2009.

Bruce, F. F. *The Spreading Flame: The Rise and Progress of Christianity from Its First Beginnings to the Conversion of the English.* Grand Rapids: Eerdmans, 1973.

Burckhardt, Jacob. *The Age of Constantine the Great.* Berkeley, California: University of California Press, 1983.

Cicero, *On the Nature of the gods, The Online Library of Liberty* (web site) Online: http://oll.libertyfund.org/?option=com_staticxt&staticfile=show.php%3Ftitle=539.

Coakley, John W., and Andrea Sterk, eds. *Readings in World Christian History.* Vol. 1, *Earliest Christianity to 1453.* Maryknoll, NY: Orbis, 2004.

Coyle, J. Kevin, "Mani, Manicheism," 520–25, in Allan Fitzgerald, ed., *Augustine Through the Ages: An Encyclopedia.* Grand Rapids, MI: Eerdmans, 1999.

Cragg, Kenneth. *The Arab Christian: A History in the Middle East.* Louisiville: John Knox, 1991.

Crosby, Cindy, and Thomas Oden. *Ancient Christian Devotional: Lectionary Cycle B.* Downers Grove, IL: InterVarsity, 2011, Kindle Edition.

Cummins, W. A. *The Age of the Picts.* Gloucester, UK: Sutton, 1995.

Cyprian, Saint. *On the Unity of the Church* in *Ante-Nicene Fathers Vol.* 5 http://www.ccel.org/ccel/schaff/anf05.iv.v.i.html/.

Decret, François, *Early Christianity in North Africa.* Translated by Edward L. Smither. Eugene, OR: Cascade Books, 2009.

Deckers, Johannes G., "Constantine the Great and Early Christian Art." *Picturing the Bible: The Earliest Christian Art,* edited by Jeffrey Spier, 87–109 New Haven: Yale University Press, 2007.

Dillenger, John. *Martin Luther: Selections from His Writings.* New York: Anchor, 1958.

Dinan, Andrew, "Manual Labor in the Life and Thought of St. Basil the Great," *Logos: A Journal of Catholic Thought and Culture* 12/4 (2009) 133–57.

Diringer, David. "The Biblical Scripts." In *The Beginnings to Jerome,* edited by P. R. Ackroyd and C. F. Evans, 11–29. The Cambridge History of the Bible 1.Cambridge: Cambridge University Press, 1970, 1989.

Dodd, C.H. *The Apostolic Preaching and Its Developments.* New York: Harper & Bros., 1936.

Ehrman, Bart D. *After the New Testament: A Reader in Early Christianity.* New York: Oxford University Press, 1998.

Elliott, John H. "Jesus the Israelite Was Neither a 'Jew' or a 'Christian': On Correcting Misleading Nomenclature." *Journal for the Study of the Historical Jesus* 5/2 (2007) 119–54.

Escobar, Samuel. *Changing Tides: Latin America & World Mission Today.* Maryknoll, NY: Orbis, 2002.

———. "Evangelical Missiology: Peering into the Future and the Turn of the Century." In *Global Missiology for the 21st Century: The Iguassu Dialogue,* edited by William D. Taylor, 101–22. Grand Rapids: Baker Academic, 2000

Eusebius. *Church History. NPNF* 2/1. *Christian Classics Ethereal Library* (web site) Online: http://www.ccel.org/ccel/schaff/npnf201.iii.viii.xxxvii.html/.

———. "Evangelism and Social Responsibility: An Evangelical Commitment," Lausanne Occasional Paper 21. Lausanne Committee for World Evangelization, 1982. Online: http://www.lausanne.org/en/documents/lops/79-lop-21.html/.

———. *History of the Martyrs in Palestine, Nicene and Post Nicene Fathers* 2:1 at *Christian Classics Ethereal Library.* Online: http://www.ccel.org/ccel/schaff/npnf201.iii. xiv.i.html/.

———. *Life of Constantine. Nicene and Post Nicene Fathers* 2:1 at *Christian Classics Ethereal Library* (web site) Online: http://www.ccel.org/ccel/schaff/npnf201.iv.vi.i.i.html/.

Evans, G. R. "Heresy, Schism." In *Augustine through the Ages: An Encyclopedia,* edited by Allan D. Fitzgerald, 424–26. Grand Rapids: Eerdmans, 1999.

Ferguson, Everett. *Church History.* Volume 1, *From Christ to Pre-Reformation: The Rise and Growth of the Church in Its Cultural, Intellectual, and Political Context.* Grand Rapids: Zondervan, 2005.

———. "Catechesis, Catechumenate." In *Encyclopedia of Early Christianity,* edited by Everett Ferguson, 223–25. London: Routledge, 1999.

———. *The Early Church at Work and Worship.* Vol. 1, *Ministry, Ordination, Covenant, and Canon.* Eugene, OR: Cascade Books, 2013.

———. *The Early Church at Work and Worship.* Vol. 2, *Catechesis, Baptism, Eschatology, and Martyrdom.* Eugene, OR: Cascade Books, 2014.

———. "Martyr, Martyrdom," In *Encyclopedia of Early Christianity,* edited by Everett Ferguson, 724–28. London: Routledge, 1999.

Fitzgerald, Allan D. *Augustine through the Ages: An Encyclopedia.* Grand Rapids: Eerdmans, 1999.

Foster, John, with W. H. C. Frend. *The First Advance, AD 29–500.* Rev. ed. Church History 1. London: SPCK, 1991.

Foster, Paul, editor. *Early Christian Thinkers: The Lives and Legacies of Twelve Key Figures.* Downers Grove, IL: IVP Academic, 2010.

———. "Tatian," In *Early Christian Thinkers: The Lives and Legacies of Twelve Key Figures,* edited by Paul Foster, 15–35. Downers Grove, IL: IVP Academic, 2010.

Fox, Robin Lane. *Pagans and Christians.* New York: HarperCollins, 1988.

Frend, W. H. C. *The Archaeology of Early Christianity: A History.* Minneapolis: Fortress, 1996.

———. *The Donatist Church: A Movement of Protest in Roman North Africa.* Oxford: Oxford University Press, 1952, 2000.

———. *Martyrdom and Persecution in the Early Church: A Study of a Conflict from the Maccabees to Donatus.* 1965. Reprinted, Grand Rapids: Baker, 1981.

———. *The Rise of Christianity.* Philadelphia: Fortress, 1984.

Bibliography

Frykenberg, R. E., "India," In *A World History of Christianity*, edited by Adrian Hastings, 147–91. Grand Rapids: Eerdmans, 1999.

Gaumer, Matthew, and Anthony DuPont, editors. *In African There Are Dissensions.* Leuven: Peeters, forthcoming.

Gehring, Roger W. *House Church and Mission: The Importance of Household Structures in Early Christianity.* Peabody, MA: Hendrickson, 2004.

Gouddard, Louis. *Christianity in Celtic Lands: A History of the Churches of the Celts, Their Development, Influence and Mutual Relations.* Dublin: Four Courts, 2004.

Green, Michael. *Evangelism in the Early Church.* Grand Rapids: Eerdmans, 1970, 2003.

Gregory, Thaumaturgus, Saint. *The Oration and Panegyric Addressed to Origen, 6.* ANF 6, Online: http://www.ccel.org/ccel/schaff/anf06.iii.iii.iv.vi.html/.

Guder, Darrell L. editor. *Missional Church: A Vision for the Sending of the Church in North America.* Grand Rapids: Eerdmans, 1998.

Hahn, Ferdinand. *Mission in the New Testament.* Translated by Frank Clarke. Studies in Biblical Theology 1/47. Naperville, IL: Allenson, 1965.

Harmless, William. editor. *Augustine in His Own Words.* Washington DC: Catholic University of America Press, 2010.

Harnack, Adolf von. *The Mission and Expansion of Christianity in the First Three Centuries,* Christian Classics Ethereal Library (web site). Online: http://www.ccel.org/ccel/harnack/mission.html/.

Hastings, Adrian. *A World History of Christianity.* Grand Rapids: Eerdmans, 1999.

Heffernan, Thomas J. *Sacred Biography: Saints and their Biographers in the Middle Ages.* Oxford: Oxford University Press, 1992.

Henderson, George and Henderson, Isabel. *The Art of the Picts: Sculpture and Metal Work in Early Medieval Scotland.* New York: Thames and Hudson, 2004.

Hesselgrave, David J. "Contextualization that this Authentic and Relevant," *International Journal of Frontier Missiology* 12/3 (1995) 115–19.

Hesselgrave, David J. *Paradigms in Conflict: 10 Key Questions in Christian Missions Today.* Grand Rapids: Kregel, 2006.

Hiebert, Paul G., "The Flaw of the Excluded Middle," *Missiology: An International Review* 10/1 (1982) 35–47.

Hinson, Glenn E. *The Church Triumphant: A History of Christianity up to 1300.* Macon, GA: Mercer University Press, 1995.

Hocking, William Ernest. *Re-thinking Missions: A Laymen's Inquiry after 100 Years.* New York: Harper and Brothers, 1932.

Holman, Susan R. *The Hungry Are Dying: Beggars and Bishops in Roman Cappadocia.* New York: Oxford University Press, 2001.

———. "The Hungry Body: Famine, Poverty, and Identity in Basil's Hom. 8." *Journal of Early Christian Studies* 7/3 (1999) 337–63.

Holmes, Michael W, editor and translator. *The Apostolic Fathers in English.* Grand Rapids: Baker Academic, 2006.

Holy Bible, English Standard Version. Wheaton, IL: Crossway, 2001.

Holy Bible, New American Standard Bible. La Habra, CA: The Lockman Foundation, 1977.

Hunter, George G. III. *The Celtic Way of Evangelism: How Christianity Can Reach the West . . . Again.* Nashville: Abingdon, 2000.

Hvalvik, Reidar, "In Word and Deed: The Expansion of the Church in the pre-Constantinian Era." In *The Mission of the Early Church to Jews and Gentiles* Jostein Adna and Hans Kvalbein, 265–87. Tübingen: Mohr/Siebeck, 2000.

"Iguassu Affirmation." In *Global Missiology for the 21st Century: The Iguassu Dialogue*, edited by William D. Taylor, 15–21. Grand Rapids: Baker Academic, 2000.

International Orality Network (web site). Online: http://www.oralbible.com/. *Interserve International* (web site). Online: http://www.interserve.org/.

Irvin, Dale T., and Scott W. Sunquist. *History of the World Christian Movement*. Vol. 1, *Earliest Christianity to 1453*. Maryknoll, NY: Orbis, 2004

Janosik, Daniel, "John of Damascus: First Apologist to the Muslims." PhD diss., Brunel University, 2010.

Jenkins, Phillip. *The Lost History of Christianity: The Thousand-Year Golden Age of the Church in the Middle East, Africa, and Asia—and How It Died*. New York: HarperOne, 2009.

Jensen, Robin M. "Early Christian Images and Exegesis." In *Picturing the Bible: The Earliest Christian Art*, edited by Jeffrey Spier, 65–85. New Haven: Yale University Press, 2007.

———. "Material Evidence (2): Visual Culture." *The Oxford Handbook of Early Christian Studies*, edited by Susan Ashbrook Harvey and David G. Hunter, 104–19. Oxford: Oxford University Press, 2008.

———. *The Substance of Things Seen: Art, Faith, and the Christian Community*. Grand Rapids: Eerdmans, 2004.

———. *Understanding Early Christian Art*. London: Routledge, 2000.

Johnson, Neal C. *Business as Mission: A Comprehensive Guide to Theory and Practice*. Downers Grove, IL: IVP Academic, 2010.

Johnson, Neal C., and Steve Rundle, "Distinctives and Challenges of Business as Mission." *Business as Mission: From Impoverished to Empowered*, edited by Tom Steffen and Mike Barnett, 19–36. Evangelical Missiological Series 14. Pasadena, CA: William Carey Library, 2006.

Julien, Tom, "The Essence of the Church," *Evangelical Missions Quarterly* 34/2 (1998). Online: http://www.emqonline.com/

Justin Martyr, Saint. *First Apology, ANF* 1. Online: http://www.ccel.org/ccel/schaff/anfo1 .viii.ii.i.html/.

———. *Second Apology, ANF* 1. Online: http://www.ccel.org/ccel/schaff/anfo1.viii.iii.i .html/.

Kalanztis, George. *Caesar and the Lamb: Early Christian Attitudes on War and Military Service*. Eugene, OR: Cascade Books, 2012.

Kelly, J. N. D. *Early Christian Doctrines*. Peabody, MA: Hendricksen, 1960, 2003.

Kessler, Herbert L., "Bright Gardens of Paradise." In *Picturing the Bible: The Earliest Christian Art*, edited by Jeffrey Spier, 111–38. New Haven: Yale University Press, 2007

Kreider, Alan. *The Change of Conversion and the Origin of Christendom*. Eugene, OR: Wipf & Stock, 1999, 2006.

———. "'They Alone Know the Right Way to Live': The Early Church and Evangelism." In *Ancient Faith for the Church's Future*, edited by Mark Husbands and Jeffrey P. Greenman, 169–86. Downers Grove, IL: IVP Academic, 2008.

Lactantius, *On the Manner in which the Persecutors Died* in *Ante-Nicene Fathers* 7 at *Christian Classics Ethereal Library* (web site) http://www.ccel.org/ccel/schaff/anfo7. iii.v.html/.

Lampe, G. W. H., editor. *The Cambridge History of the Bible*. Vol. 2, *The West from the Fathers to the Reformation*. Cambridge: Cambridge University Press, 1969, 1989.

Lampe, Peter. *From Paul to Valentinus: Christians at Rome in the First Two Centuries.* Translated by Michael Steinhauser. Edited by Marshall D. Johnson. Minneapolis: Fortress, 2003.

Larkin, William J., and Joel F. Williams. *Mission in the New Testament: An Evangelical Approach.* Maryknoll, NY: Orbis, 1998.

Latourette, Kenneth Scott. *A History of the Expansion of Christianity: The First Five Centuries.* Grand Rapids: Zondervan, 1938, 1966.

"The Lausanne Covenant," *The Lausanne Movement* (website). Online: http://www .lausanne.org/en/gatherings/issue-based/easneye-1986.html?id=26

Leithart, Peter J. *Defending Constantine: The Twilight of an Empire and the Dawn of Christendom.* Downers Grove, IL: IVP Academic, 2010.

Little, Christopher, "What Makes Mission Christian?" *International Journal of Frontier Missiology* 25/2 (2008) 65–73.

MacMullen, Ramsay. *Christianity and Paganism in the Fourth to Eighth Centuries.* New Haven: Yale University Press, 1999.

————. *Christianizing the Roman Empire (A.D. 100–400).* New Haven: Yale University Press, 1984.

————. *Constantine.* New York: Dial Press, 1969.

Margolis, Max L. *The Story of Bible Translations.* Philadelphia: Jewish Publication Society of America, 1917.

Marshall, I. Howard, "Who were the Evangelists?" In *The Mission of the Early Church to Jews and Gentiles,* edited by Jostein Adna and Hans Kvalbein, 251–63. Tübingen: Mohr/Siebeck, 2000.

Marty, Martin. *Martin Luther: A Life.* London: Penguin, 2008,

McDay, Dominique, "Missionary Heather Mercer Tells Story of Captivity in Afghanistan." Liberty University (website). Online: http://www.liberty.edu/index .cfm?PID=18495&MID=5002/.

McHugh, Michael P., "Cappadocia." In *Encyclopedia of Early Christianity,* edited by Everett Ferguson, 213–15. London: Routledge, 1999.

McKnight, Scott. *The King Jesus Gospel: The Original Good News Revisited.* Grand Rapids: Zondervan, 2011.

McQuilkin, Robertson et al. "Responses to Christopher Little's 'What Makes Mission Christian?'" *International Journal of Frontier Missiology* 25/2 (2008) 75–85.

Medearis, Carl. *Speaking of Jesus: The Art of Non-Evangelism.* Colorado Springs: Cook, 2011.

Meehan, Bernard. *The Book of Kells: An Illustrated Introduction to the Manuscript in Trinity College Dublin.* London: Thames & Hudson, 1995.

Meier, John. *A Marginal Jew.* Vol. 3, *Rethinking the Historical Jesus.* New York: Doubleday, 1994, 2001.

Merdinger, Jane, "Do You Renounce Satan and All His Works? Successes and Failures amongst the Catechumenate in Late Roman Africa," Online: people.vanderbilt. edu/~james.p.burns/chroma/baptism/merbapt.html/.

Metzger, Bruce M. *The Bible in Translation: Ancient and English Versions.* Grand Rapids, MI: Baker Academic, 2001.

————. *The Early Versions of the New Testament: Their Origin, Transmission, and Limi tations.* Oxford: Clarendon, 1977, 2001.

Miller, David L. "Mission-Minded Latinos No Longer Staying at Home." *Christianity Today.* December 8, 1997.

Minns, Denis, "Irenaeus." In *Early Christian Thinkers: The Lives and Legacies of Twelve Key Figures*, edited by Paul Foster, 36–51. Downers Grove, IL: IVP Academic, 2010.

"Mission to Intellectuals," *Time Magazine*, January 11, 1960, 62–63.

Moffett, Samuel. *A History of Christianity in Asia*. Vol. 1, *Beginnings to 1500*. New York: HarperCollins, 1992.

Moon, Ruth, "Why Evangelical Leaders Love Pope Benedict XVI (And His Resignation)," *Christianity Today* February 13, 2013. Online: http://www.christianitytoday.com/ct/2013/february-web-only/why-evangelical-leaders-love-pope-benedict-xvi.html/.

Moreau, A. Scott. *Contextualization in World Missions: Mapping and Assessing Evangelical Models*. Grand Rapids: Kregel, 2012.

Moreau, A. Scott et al. *Introducing World Missions: A Biblical, Historical, and Practical Survey*. Grand Rapids: Baker Academic, 2004.

Moss, Candida. *Ancient Christian Martyrdom: Diverse Practices, Theologies, and Traditions*. New Haven: Yale University Press, 2012.

Muers, Rachel, "Adoptionism: Is Jesus Christ the Son of God by Nature or by Adoption?" In *Heresies and How to Avoid Them: Why It Matters What Christians Believe*, edited by Ben Quash and Michael Ward, 50–58. Peabody, MA: Hendricksen, 2007.

Mursurillo, Herbert. *Acts of the Christian Martyrs*. Oxford: Oxford University Press, 1999.

Neill, Stephen. *A History of Christian Missions*. London: Penguin, 1964, 1990.

Newbign, Leslie. *The Open Secret: An Introduction to the Theology of Mission*. Grand Rapids: Eerdmans, 1995.

Newman, John Henry. *Rise and Progress of Universities and Benedictine Essays*. Notre Dame, IN: University of Notre Dame Press, 2001.

Noll, Mark A. *Turning Points: Decisive Moments in the History of Christianity*. 3rd ed. Grand Rapids: Baker, 2012.

Oden, Thomas C. *The African Memory of Mark: Reassessing Early Church Tradition*. Downers Grove, IL: IVP Academic, 2011.

———. *Early Libyan Christianity: Uncovering a North African Tradition*. Downers Grove, IL: IVP Academic, 2011.

———. *How Africa Shaped the Christian Mind: Rediscovering the African Seedbed of Western Christianity*. Downers Grove, IL: IVP Books, 2007.

O'Loughlin, Thomas. *Discovering Saint Patrick*. Mahwah, NJ: Paulist, 2004.

———. *Saint Patrick: The Man and His Works*. London: Triangle, 1999.

Orality Strategies (web site). Online: https://www.oralitystrategies.org/

Osiek, Carolyn, and and David L. Balch. *Families in the New Testament World: Households and House Churches*. Louisville: Westminster/John Knox, 1997.

Osiek, Carolyn, and Margaret Y. MacDonald, with Janet Tulloch. *A Woman's Place: House Churches in Earliest Christianity*. Minneapolis: Fortress, 2006.

Parvis, Paul, "Justin Martyr." In *Early Christian Thinkers: The Lives and Legacies of Twelve Key Figures*, edited by 1–14. Downers Grove, IL: IVP Academic, 2010.

Parvis, Sara, "Perpetua." In *Early Christian Thinkers: The Lives and Legacies of Twelve Key Figures*, 100–110. Downers Grove, IL: IVP Academic, 2010.

Parvis, Sara, and Paul Foster, editors. *Justin Martyr and His Worlds*. Minneapolis: Fortress, 2007.

Patitsas, Timothy, "St. Basil's Philanthropic Program and Modern Microlending Strategies for Economic Self-Actualization." In *Wealth and Poverty in Early Church and Society*, edited by Susan R. Holman 267–86. Grand Rapids: Baker Academic, 2008.

Bibliography

Patzia, Arthur G. *The Making of the New Testament: Origin, Collection, Text & Canon.* Downers Grove, IL: Intervarsity Press, 1995, 2011.

Paul VI, Pope. *Verbum Dei: Dogmatic Constitution on Divine Revelation,* November 18, 1965 at *Vatican* (web site). Online: http://www.vatican.va/archive/hist_councils/ii_vatican_council/documents/vat-ii_const_19651118_dei-verbum_en.html/.

Perler, Othmar. *Les Voyages de Saint Augustin.* Paris: Etudes Augustiniennes, 1969.

"Pew Research Center: Publications," February 16, 2011, *Pew Research Center* (website). Online: http://pewresearch.org/pubs/1770/ask-the-expert-pew-research-center/.

Piper, John. *Let the Nations Be Glad: The Supremacy of God in Missions.* Grand Rapids: Baker Academic, 1996, 2010.

PMI USA (web site). Online: http://www.pmi-usa.org.

Ramsey, Boniface. *Beginning to Read the Fathers.* Mahwah, NJ: Paulist, 1985.

Riddle, Donald Wayne, "Early Christian Hospitality: A Factor in the Gospel Transmission," *Journal of Biblical Literature* 57/2 (1938) 141–54.

Robert, Dana L. *Christian Mission: How Christianity Became a World Religion.* Oxford: Wiley-Blackwell, 2009.

Rogers, Rick, "Theophilus of Antioch." *Early Christian Thinkers: The Lives and Legacies of Twelve Key Figures,* edited by Paul Foster, 52–67. Downers Grove, IL: IVP Academic, 2010.

Rothschild, Clare K., and Jens Schröter, eds. *The Rise and Expansion of Christianity in the First Three Centuries of the Common Era.* Wissenschaftliche Untersuchungen zum Neuen Testament 31. Tübingen: Mohr/Siebeck, 2013.

Rousseau, Phillip. *Basil of Caesarea.* Berkley: University of California Press, 1998.

Rundle, Stephen L., and Tom Steffen. *Great Commission Companies: The Emerging Role of Business in Missions.* Downers Grove, IL: Intervarsity, 2003.

Russell, Mark, "Christian Mission is Holistic." *International Journal of Frontier Missiology* 25/2 (2008) 93–98.

Sanneh, Lamin. *Translating the Message: The Missionary Impact on Culture.* Maryknoll, NY: Orbis, 2009.

Schnabel, Eckhard, *Early Christian Mission: Paul and the Early Church.* Vol. 2, DownersGrove, IL: Intervarsity Press, 2004.

Smith, Carl, "Post-Bauer Scholarship on Gnosticism(s): The Current State of Our 'Knowledge,'" unpublished paper given at the Evangelical Theological Society, San Francisco, CA, November 17, 2011.

Smither, Edward. "Augustine, a Missionary to Heretics? An Appraisal of Augustine's Missional Engagement with the Donatists." In *In Africa There Are Dissensions,* edited by Matthew Gaumer and Anthony DuPont,. Leuven: Peeters, 2014.

Smither, Edward. *Augustine as Mentor: A Model for Preparing Spiritual Leaders.* Nashville: B&H, 2008.

———. "Basil of Caesarea: An Early Christian Model of Urban Mission." In *Reaching the City: Reflections on Mission for the 21st Century,* edited by Gary Fujino et al., 77–95. Pasadena, CA: William Carey Library, 2012.

———. *Brazilian Evangelical Missions in the Arab World: History, Culture, Practice, and Theology.* Eugene, OR: Pickwick Publications, 2012.

———. "Did the Rise of Constantine Mean the End of Christian Mission?" In *Rethinking Constantine: History, Theology, Legacy,* edited by Edward Smither, . Eugene, OR: Pickwick Publications, 2014

————. "Lessons from a Tentmaking Ascetic in the Egyptian Desert: The Case of Evagrius of Pontus," *Missiology: An International Review* 39/4 (2011) 485–96.

————, "'To Emulate and Imitate': Possidius' Life of Augustine as a FifthCentury Discipleship Tool." *Southwestern Journal of Theology* 50/2 (2008) 146–66.

————. "Reflections on Patristic Evangelism and Discipleship," In *The Contemporary Church and the Early Church: Case Studies in Ressourcement*, edited by Paul Hartog, 27–49. Evangelical Theological Society Monograph Series. Eugene, OR: Pickwick Publications, 2010.

Sordi, Marta. *The Christians and the Roman Empire*. Norman: University of Oklahoma Press, 1994.

Spier, Jeffrey, editor. *Picturing the Bible: The Earliest Christian Art*. New Haven: Yale University Press, 2007.

Stark, Rodney. *The Rise of Christianity: A Sociologist Reconsiders History*. Princeton: Princeton University Press, 1997.

Sterk, Andrea. *Renouncing the World Yet Leading the Church: The Monk-Bishop in Late Antiquity*. Cambridge: Harvard University Press, 2004.

Stevenson, James. *The New Eusebius: Documents Illustrative of the Church to A.D. 337*. London: SPCK, 1957.

Sulpitius Severus, *Life of St. Martin*, NPNF 2:11. Online: http://www.ccel.org/ccel/schaff/npnf211.ii.ii.html/.

Sweet, John, "Docetism: Is Jesus Christ Really Human or Did He Just Appear to Be So?" In *Heresies and How to Avoid Them: Why It Matters What Christians Believe*, edited by Ben Quash and Michael Ward, 24–31. Peabody, MA: Hendrickson, 2007.

Tertullian. *Apology*. ANF 3. Online: http://www.ccel.org/ccel/schaff/anf03.iv.iii.xxxvii.html/.

————. *To Scapula*, Ante-Nicene Fathers 3.Online: http://www.ccel.org/ccel/schaff/anf03.iv.vii.v.html/.

"The People Next Door," Lausanne Occasional Paper 55. Lausanne Committee for World Evangelization, 2005. Online: http://www.lausanne.org/documents/2004forum/LOP55_IG26.pdf/.

Thomas, Charles. *Christianity in Roman Britain to AD 500*. Berkeley: University of California Press, 1981.

Thomas, George, "Malatya Martyrs: Oaks of Righteousness." *CBN News*, website. Online: http://www.cbn.com/cbnnews/world/2007/May/Malatya-Martyrs-Oaks-of-Righteousness/.

Thompson, Glenn. "From Sinner to Saint? Seeking a Consistent Constantine." In *Rethinking Constantine: History, Theology, Legacy*, edited by Edward Smither. Eugene, OR: Pickwick Publications, forthcoming.

Tucker, Ruth. *From Jerusalem to Irian Jaya: A Biographical History of Christian Missions*. Grand Rapids: Zondervan, 2004.

Tunehag, Mats et al., editors. "Business as Mission," Lausanne Occasional Paper 59. Lausanne Committee for World Evangelization, 2005. Online: http://www.lausanne.org/documents/2004forum/LOP59_IG30.pdf/.

Van Dam, Raymond. *The Roman Revolution of Constantine*. Cambridge: Cambridge University Press, 2008.

Walls Andrew F. *The Missionary Movement in Christian History: Studies in the Transmission of Faith*. Maryknoll, NY: Orbis, 1996.

Ward, Benedicta, and G. R. Evans. "The Medieval West." In *A World History of Christianity*, edited by Adrian Hastings, 110–46. Grand Rapids: Eerdmans, 1999.

Ward, Kevin, "Africa." In *A World History of Christianity*, edited by Adrian Hastings, 192–237. Grand Rapids: Eerdmans, 1999.

Willis, Avery et al. Making Disciples of Oral Learners. Lausanne Occasional Paper 54. Online: http://www.lausanne.org/docs/2004forum/LOP54_IG25.pdf

Wilken, Robert L. *The First Thousand Years: A Global History of Christianity*. New Haven: Yale University Press, 2012.

"Wycliffe: Our History." *Wycliffe*. Online: http://www.wycliffe.org/About/OurHistory.aspx

"Wycliffe: Translation Statistics." *Wycliffe*. Online: http://www.wycliffe.org/About/Statistics.aspx/.

Yarnold, Edward. *The Awe-Inspiring Rites of Initiation: The Origins of the R.C.I.A.* Collegeville, MN: Liturgical, 1994, 2001.

Index

Alopen, 42, 113
Antioch of Syria, 8–9, 12, 15, 17, 33, 35, 42, 50, 81, 93, 131, 148, 154
Arabia, 14, 27, 42, 125
Arian; Arianism, 15, 20, 26, 28, 35, 102, 133–34
Armenia, 2, 13, 22, 30, 82, 93, 95, 103–5, 133, 138
Armenian Scriptures, 103–5
Athenagoras, 68, 80, 112–13
Augustine of Canterbury, 11, 22, 36–37, 41, 84, 114–17, 125–26, 157
Augustine of Hippo, 19, 25–27, 33–34, 40, 45, 68, 70–71, 77–80, 86–88, 90, 96–99, 103, 107, 112–13, 133–34, 140, 159–62

Basil of Caesarea, 34, 40, 129, 132–40, 143, 146–47, 162, 165
basileas, 137–39, 147
basilicas, 149–51, 155–56, 158, 162–63
Bede, 11, 37, 40–41, 60–61, 71, 83, 114–15
Boniface, 22–23, 36, 41–42, 116–17
Book of Kells, 41, 97, 121–23
Buddhism; Buddhist, 42, 113, 116, 124, 165

catechesis; catechumens, 76, 159–62
Charles Martel, 23, 42, 117
China, 14, 25, 36, 42–43, 94, 113, 118, 123, 130

Clement of Alexandria, 11, 24, 30, 38, 81
Columba, 35–36, 40–41, 83–84, 90, 118–19, 122, 130, 144–47, 165
Columban, 36, 40–41, 83, 100
Constantine, 2, 9, 15, 18–24, 50, 62, 82, 102, 105, 114, 141, 149–51, 155–56, 158, 162–63
Coptic Scriptures, 93, 100–101, 107, 125
Council of Chalcedon, 26, 42, 85
Council of Nicaea, 14–15, 31, 26
Cyprian of Carthage, 10–12, 18, 25, 45, 50, 54, 70–71, 96, 162

Decius, 17–18, 43
Didache, 31, 46, 160–61
Diocletian, 18, 43–44, 55, 63, 76
Donatists, 20–21, 27, 86–88

Edessa, 2, 12–13, 42, 93, 104, 131–32
Ephraem of Syria, 13, 131
Ethiopia, 14, 26, 105–7
Ethiopic Scriptures, 93, 105–7
Eusebius of Caesarea, 10–12, 19–21, 30–32, 38, 44, 56–67, 63–66, 81, 85
evangelism, 1, 3–4, 74–77, 82, 85, 89–90, 100, 110–11, 124, 128, 132, 146–47, 159, 162

Galerius, 18–19
Georgian Scriptures, 93, 95, 105

Gnosticism, 11, 24–25, 34, 39, 58, 81, 85–86

Gothic Scriptures, 93, 102–3

Goths, 15, 18, 26, 28, 133, 138

Gregory, Bishop of Rome, 36–38, 41, 72, 114–17, 126, 157

Gregory Thaumaturgus, 9, 34–35, 39, 134, 139, 143–46, 159

Gregory the Enlightener, 13, 82, 103

house churches, 13, 149–55, 162–63

Ignatius of Antioch, 33, 35, 50, 57–58, 93

India, 13–14, 30–31, 35, 38, 81, 94

Irenaeus of Lyon, 10, 24, 34–35, 57–58, 85–86, 96, 140–41, 160–61

Islam, 5, 15–16, 23–25, 42, 88–89, 101, 107, 125, 141, 165

Jerome, 30, 96–99, 103, 106

Jews; Judaism, 9, 17, 20, 25, 27, 38, 50, 56–57, 90, 95, 126, 149

John of Damascus, 86, 88–89

Justin Martyr, 10, 20, 25, 35, 38, 43, 54, 57–59, 67–68, 73, 77, 80–82, 85, 111–13, 126, 140, 147

Latin Vulgate, 96–100, 103, 107–8, 121

Martin of Tours, 34–35, 133, 143, 144, 146, 162, 165

martyrs; martyrdom, 2, 9, 16, 23, 25, 33, 35–36, 45, 47, 49, 51–67, 69–73, 82, 93

miracles, 35, 41, 140–47

missio Dei, 2, 5, 92, 166

missionary monks, 11, 14, 22, 32, 36–37, 39–47, 83–85, 113–15, 118–19, 122, 124, 126, 129–30, 138, 157, 162, 165

Nestorians, 14, 26, 36, 42–43, 94, 113, 118, 123–26, 130

North Africa, 2, 12, 23, 25, 45–47, 52–53, 63, 87, 96, 98, 102, 107–8, 125, 152

Old Latin Bible, 95–99, 101, 121

Origen, 11, 32, 34–35, 38–39, 43, 46, 57, 81–82, 98, 111, 126

Pantaenus, 11, 35, 38, 81

Patrick of Ireland, 11, 22, 35–37, 82–83, 90, 125, 156, 162

Paul, Apostle, 7–11, 14, 16, 47, 50, 75, 77–78, 89–90, 98, 149, 153–54, 166

Perpetua and Felicitas, 2, 25, 53–54, 56, 59, 61, 64–65, 70, 159

Pictish art, 118–19, 121–22, 126,

Picts, 40, 83, 118–19, 121–22, 126, 144–45

Pliny, govenor of Bithynia, 2, 9, 16–17, 43, 76

Polycarp, 9, 16, 33, 35, 53–54, 56, 66, 69–70, 86

proclamation, 3–5, 30, 74–76, 86, 89, 93, 127–28, 139, 141, 143, 145–46, 156, 159, 166

sacred biographies, 69, 71–73, 101, 144

St. Martin's Cross, 119–22

Syriac Scriptures, 93–96, 101, 107

Tertullian, 10–12, 19, 24, 43, 45, 58–59, 68–69, 73, 76, 82, 96, 112, 159

Tiridates, king of Armenia, 13, 22, 82, 103

Trajan, 2, 16–17, 67

Ulfilas, 15, 26, 28, 102

Valerian, 18, 43–44, 76

Zoroastrianism, 25, 165